MW00416904

AMERICAN MUTT BARKS IN THE YARD

DAVID BARRINGER

EMIGRE NO. 68

CO-PUBLISHED BY PRINCETON ARCHITECTURAL PRESS, 2005.

Designed and edited by Rudy VanderLans with David Barringer.
Copy editing by Nick Wright/Alice Polesky.

Emigre, 1700 Shattuck Ave., #307, Berkeley, California 94709
Visit our web site at www.emigre.com.

Co-published by Princeton Architectural Press
37 East Seventh Street
New York, New York 10003
For a free catalog of books, call 1.800.722.6657.
Visit our Web site at www.papress.com.

© 2005 Emigre, Inc.
All rights reserved

Printed and bound in Canada in an edition of 4,000 copies.

06 05 04 5 4 3 2 1 First edition

No part of this publication may be used or reproduced
in any manner without written permission from the publisher,
except in the context of reviews.

ISBN 1-56898-486-3
ISSN 1045-3717

APOLOGY. I am a self-taught graphic designer, which means I resent the teacher. What does he know that I don't? I don't think he knows, half the time, what he's talking about. He flips through design mags, surfs the web, trolls the library stacks, gets an "idea," becomes "inspired," and off he goes, assigning me some task he can't explain—he apologizes for his inarticulate stammering—and, after an hour or two of driving my wet nose into the pages of Photoshop and InDesign2 manuals, he elbows me aside, takes the mouse by the infrared tail, and leaves me snubbed, shamed and rolled-newspaper-swatted. I am jittery with bloodlust, gnashing intonations that begin with *righteous* and end with *mayhem*, aflame with the heat of a wrathful Cain't unto his unbrotherly unAbel.

Even now he begs me to drop this conceit—*drop it!*—warning me that I can't possibly sustain this false metosis (the autobiology of self division) for an entire essay (or assay).

Ask me what it feels like to apprentice beneath a mentor who has lost faith in you. Go ahead. Ask me. I know this one.

DEFINITION. To be self-taught is to:
- never trust the teacher & so never mistake the lesson for the final word;
- be always humble in the skin of one's knowledge & modest in the suit of one's skill;
- toil in the shadow of self-doubt, for the teacher lacks the authority to confer a passing grade on the pupil.

DESCRIPTION. To be self-taught is to learn by doing. Passion motivates the learning. The desire to create starts every sentence with "I want": *I want to do this; so I want to learn*

how to do this. To create, I must know. To know, I must
want to know. The end is in sight before the beginning is
felt. This leap of imagination is Desire bounding a canyon,
seeking the opposite bank, then backpedaling in midair
like a cartoon character struck by a late understanding:
I must first build a bridge.

The project (to make this or that) gives purpose to the
study (to learn how). I am a writer, photographer, and erst-
while lawyer. I have no formal training in photography,
writing, or design, not even a seminar in Vegas or a conference in Miami. Here I am, a mongrel leering at the fat leg of
Design. I have written a book, say, and I want to design a
book cover. I browse book covers at library and bookstore,
flip through my kids' artwork, take a hacksaw to a slab of
pine. (This is what I love about design: anything's fair
game. Photography, collage, sketches, type. I can sledge-
hammer an old TV if I want to. I can paint my penis blue.
I can write a short story to fit the bookmark I'm designing.
Whatever.) I reject the first dozen ideas as too obvious,
literal or uninteresting. I consider what books do, how
they feel, regard them, alternately, as objects and as con-
veyances of information. I flatter myself into thinking I'm
deconstructing "bookness" when really I'm staring into
space thinking about sex. I check out books on the craft of
bookmaking, and then I literally tear one apart, dissecting
the spine and the fascia of glue. I try not to think about
C. Kidd. Also, I place books in weird places—on the fridge,
under the car, in a bush—and I sneak up and scare them,
hoping to hear them exclaim. Eventually, I get an idea.

If the idea involves illustration, I teach myself to illustrate. I open up Illustrator, which I got from work, and the
program crashes when I caress the first tool, and I'm too

scared to reopen it. I run to Photoshop and illustrate in vectors. Awkward but I get the job done. Oh, I gotta buy those Pantone things with all the colors on them. Every time I want to do something, I have to use the online Help or thumb one of three manuals. This is distracting, as investigation leads to investigation, tool is related to tool, I've forgotten the White Rabbit because I'm too busy getting bigger and smaller, running to stand still, and it's hours before I learn the one thing I wanted to learn, but along the way I've learned umpteen other things, including several ways to place the image into InDesign. And so on until, finger-cramped and mind-sopped, I have my book cover. The whole process is like an upended pyramid, a factory built to produce a single button, a body cultivated for its hair, a sentence whose only visible character is the period. Inefficient, bloated, digressive, backward, but driven from the start with fuel to burn and, through it all to the end, so goddamn satisfying it's like days of foreplay dramatizing The History of Foreplay leading up to the Big Finish, the orgasm, the creation, the Big Bang, my finished design, my little insect, bug of my loins: *Crawl, Baby! Skitter! Fly! Flit!*

All is well until Perspective leaves the window unlocked and Reason climbs in like a thief in the night and snatches my smug dream-bubbles of *You the man!* and *Damn, I'm good*—and out the window floats Reason clutching my helium bouquet of Pride to the tune of "No One Likes a Showoff" sung by the bird choir of the Aesthetic Vendettas, whose first big hit was "Oh, Take Your Myopic Self-Involvement and Shove It Up Your Asterisk," and I wake up to face this music of recrimination, this dawn of second thoughts, and lo, there it is, my book cover, not so damn hot after all, and behold, here I am, not so damn close to a likeness of a god as I'd hoped. The gratification has worn off, like the effects of champagne, like silly bubbles I am ashamed of having mistaken for gems.

Bad dog. Bad bad dog.

Start again.

And haven't I already started again, haven't I already grown, in one night, gone from smitten amateur to brutal critic? As long as I love what I'm doing and hate what I've done, I figure I'm on a right track. Or a tight rack. Either way, I'm being stretched in limbward directions, wrenched in the torso by opposing tendon-cies.

Every new project is another occasion for study, another history lesson, another exercise in learning that I don't know nothing.

Start, start again.

And I do.

My greatest fear is not to fail; it is to fail to notice that I've failed. I will never admit allegiance with those people for whom the ubiquity of software devalues the contributions of graphic designers, those nebbishes for whom *"Can't I do that myself on Word?"* isn't a question, it's an answer that ends the conversation.

Sure, you can—if you want it to look like crap.

DISCLOSURE. I have a day job. In this day job, I run a corporate (the client is technically non-profit) magazine: I take photos, write the articles, and either art-direct the magazine or sit and do the layouts myself. When I'm not doing this, I'm doing other projects: books, booklets, brochures, posters, etc. I confess for two reasons.

(1) My job provides me with the tools I am thus able to

employ in my own off-hours home-office pursuits. This means I am subsidized. No way could I have otherwise afforded the hardware, the software, the time to observe and learn the businesses of design, prepress and printing. This is not to say that I have not sacrificed salary for the flexibility of working part-time. This is to say, however, that I did not walk out the door one day and concoct this set-up from scratch (it took years of flailing around in the sea of debt and despair, which sounds melodramatic and probably is, today, but it didn't feel like it back then) and also to say that I recognize that my way is my way and I don't have the least interest in identifying some kind of silly work-life trend others may replicate. I have not, in my boss, who knows some of what I do, an unwilling patron of my arts. I've never been a full-time employee, never had benefits except the most important one: TIME, time to raise my kids[1] and pursue my projects. I am lucky. If you are not lucky, be discreet.

(2) My self-education is neither unmotivated by profit nor unrelated to my day job. As a corollary: my off-hours projects are neither (a) profitable, despite my intents, nor (b) always soul-satisfying, despite my creative control, with (a) and (b) being realities familiar to any kid running a lemonade stand: a long day on a hot curb may as capriciously crush as ennoble the entrepreneurial spirit.

IMPASSIONED GRAPHIC DESIGN. 50¢

OBSERVATION. Obsessions are not economically rational.

WHAT DO I THINK I'M DOING. Art is an expression of hope. In other words, a delusion, a denial of what is likely, a willing disregard of probabilities. Reckless defiance. An assertion of self against the odds.

Q: What artists inspire you the most?

A: The dead ones. They inspire me to work faster.

DISCLOSURE, PART II. It was by immersion in the design world that I, as a writer and photographer, came to regard its wonders, covet its powers, and envy its practitioners. I was around it (as if I were in a bathysphere lowered into the deep sea, observant but untouched) for over five years before I figured it wouldn't hurt to learn a little of this stuff and keep my projects moving when the desks in the prepress department teetered with towers of job tickets. I was already art-directing magazines and books (a green civilian literally back-seat driving over the cold shoulders of veteran designers), but I was limited by my ignorance of what was possible. So about a year ago I entered the control room and started flipping switches in Photoshop and spinning knobs in PageMaker. My latent desires came to the surface. I loved this stuff. I loved the control. I loved the instant gratification. It felt like writing felt: I was making real on the page what was only, moments before, a synaptic phantom in my head.

In college during the late Eighties, I'd spent night after night at the computer lab changing the fonts, paragraphs, columns, and margins of my essays and stories. The user interface of the Macintosh IIC introduced me to the drop-down menu and the strange vocabulary of *Font, Superscript, Leading, Indent.* Sensitive instantly to the influence type and spacing had on the experience of reading, and thus unable to bear another term paper double-spaced in 12-point Courier, I'd mess around with my stories to the grave dismay of professors and peers who chided me for vanity. I was told to keep to my place and stick to what I knew. I was guilty of self-consciousness, of, essentially, self-publishing. Thinking about the look of my words on the page was about as shallow as one could get (at least for those of us students not in the art school).

I suppose, today, strict formatting rules save professors from the eye strain of reading twenty-page essays set in 14-point Beesknees or 10-point Curlz, but, strangely, you'd think that people, by now, would be better at typesetting, that the everywhereness of computers, word-processing software, and font libraries would improve our collective sense of design. This is as naïve a thought as the expectation that letting people loose in the mall would somehow guarantee that the fashions at the food court would rival those on the runways of Paris. On the contrary, intoxicated by novelty, users tend to get a little crazy, lifting up the shirts of their font menus and, as desperate for attention as Spring Breakers on *Girls Gone Wild*, letting it all hang out. This is good news for graphic designers anxious about their job security. Software alone a designer does not make.

Fifteen years later, I now find I'm adopting the chilly mien of my old college professors by chastening clients who presume to tell me my job. I advise them, euphemistically, of course, to keep to their place and stick to what they know. This is great irony considering that I myself am a party-crasher who now presumes to check IDs at the door, a savage in a rented tux.

OPPORTUNISM. So I have a day job; also, I work in the off hours, doing projects I want to do but don't yet know how to do, thus expanding the zones in which I am dull or dangerous. No one ever said The Job was the be all, end all, and if they did, they were trying to hire you. If they said you're the only one who can do this particular job, they were flattering your ego in lieu of raising your salary. Meritocracy is dead. Have you heard this, too? All you need to get and keep a job is a level of competency and a feel for bluff. To move ahead, to rise, well, that's the altitude at which the lungs of merit fail. Careerism has nothing to do with excellence in a craft or transcendence in an art; it has everything to do with notoriety in a society or sub-set thereof. The politics of opportunism. The bloodluck of nepotism. The pressurized cabin of privilege. The cruel math of cronyism. It is here, languishing in a stagnant cubicle, that the thirtysomething idealist appreciates the original sin committed in college: it would have been far better to have forgone attentiveness to grades and stood up, walked over to the son of the CEO, the daughter of the trustee, the nephew of the judge, and shook hands. Was it such a long way, looking back, to go from here to affinity? And isn't the price of inaction too steep? Look around you. It's never too late. Try again. Join a club. Play golf. Put on a false face, pretend to care, and say hello.

SECRET WORK. Meanwhile, I have saved myself the heart-break and taken it as given that my job, by definition, will never satisfy me. I don't surrender. I don't check my self-respect at the door. A jellyfish from eight to six I am not. I am the same person by day as by night, after all, and Batman can apply Bruce Wayne's newly acquired know-how as usefully as Bruce Wayne can apply Batman's. Ideally, each informs the other, like neighbors exchanging recipes and gossip.

The secret work I have in mind is not a spiteful indulgence that dodges the question of how to improve one's practice of design. It is, plainly stated, work you love to do, and you get to do it with as few strings attached as possible. Besides, your off-hours muscles need not remain a secret. Bruce Wayne can wear tight shirts and fight crime, too, on his own terms. It's just that everybody knows Batman is free to kick ass for only two people: Lady Justice, and himself. Secret work, working off-hours, working for yourself—however you want to word it or fit the circumstances to your needs—is liberating in the best sense I can think of: the personal sense. Without the hands of the free, there is no home of the brave.

I deploy the superhero analogy to temper the designer's old bipolar personality type, the servant/rebel. We all know, by now, that graphic designers, like lawyers, like others in the service industries, are organ grinder's monkeys dancing for coin, not knights of the realm lancing for honor. To rejoice, without reservation, in one's servant status is to embrace a slave mentality, a masochism as rewarded in the cubicle, I suppose, as on the pew or oarsman's bench. Truth is a stinky lotion, but you don't have to rub it in.

Instead, I am reasonable in my expectations of the fit of my heart into the vise of my job. Look beyond the glass walls for love, my friend. Every day is a day for secret work you can put your secret heart into and make something big and grand and noble. Or else something small and personal and dignified. You're miserable most of the time anyway. Try this, the secret work we do outside the zoo. After hours, when the animals roam free, we owe no one the wages of our domesticity. Exit cage left, and you'll find the cost of entry into the world of secrets and deception is nearly as low as the cost of your free time.

ROMANCE. The cost of entry: meaning, the cost of the cardboard box of your computer, the hand-scrawled sign of your website or printed pulp, the lemonade of your creations—when has it ever been more possible for a chimp like you to walk to the end of your driveway and stake a claim? Your grandpa has a website, for the love of Henry Ford, and your niece has a zine, for the worship of Hilary Duff. And the wonderful thing about graphic design is that, like writing, you don't need a team; you can grab your sketchbook or boot your laptop and go Hand Solo. Plus, how many cheap online digital-press shops are there; how many silkscreeners with beard crumbs and Nader pins; how many lithographers with regrets to exorcise and busted dirt bikes to fix? And they're all waiting to produce your projects. For once, you can come up with the product, not just the packaging; the service, not just the logo. Compared to Gutenberg, you're Optimus Prime, RAM-hearted, wireless, and limbed by Hewlett-Packard. Don't waste the moment. Don't sneer at the romance. Don't kill the mood just as the clothes hit the floor. Get naked. Procreate.

ENERGY + WILL. Okay, so, once you have the tools (from work or courtesy of your holiday checks), you need energy and will: health and restlessness, anger and melancholy.[†] Life sucks, but you're still alive. Now what? Relieve yourself of the miseries of existence and the givens of your formulaic life and do something. You can't fail if you don't

---

† My college English professor (John Rubadeau) to this day paraphrases a quote from Leonardo da Vinci, that genius is energy plus will—talent being the factor expressly excluded from this formula (luckily, for most of us).

hate the winners. Hate them. Avenge your pitiful life. And feel your energy surge like a sword levitating off the wall, across the room, and into your hand. Too male for you? Fine. Insert the blue skies and daisies of your own analogy and get to work. Just don't tell your coworkers. They will rat. They will turn your life of the mind into a life of the mine field and make you beg for a life of mind-your-own-business.

GOOD HARD WORK. Energy? Check. Furious will? Check. Ramming your head into the wall over and over again? On it. And while you brush the brick dust from your noodle, ask yourself how does it hurt, why does it hurt, and will it hurt differently next time? Quantify and qualify the hurt's dynamics, its context and meaning, to wit: *life is pain; suffering is the story of our times; I'm a bloody idiot.* Good hard work will sweep the crusted scabs of analysis out of your skullcase, leaving you headroom to concentrate on nothing but the urgency of your eye-level task. You'll love what work does for you. The lack of it will drive you mad. You'll become addicted to it. You'll have to; only an addict would keep at it like this, you crazy bastard. I salute you.[2]

JANUS, GOD OF THEORY. And when the work is done, and Perspective unlocks the window, and Reason sneaks in like a thief in the night, I am reminded that, just like writing is rewriting, designing is redesigning. I look at my work, my orphan, I weep for her fate, I summon phrases like "the mob rules the marketplace" and "the consolation of theory," and I revalue where I have been and rechart where I am going.

Theory is two-faced like Janus, with two agendas: to memorialize a lost war or to justify a victory. And with daily battles in the marketplace of ideas, Janus is a busy god, as liable to be consulted by craftspeople as capitalists. *Does what happened matter? Is what's happening ominous?*

As the experts and professionals, the employed and sub-contracted, we are advised (by our employers, marketplace dictates, economic realities) against crossing the street of possibility and invited to just stand and hold hands and look every which way but down. Root for a team, if you must —an army of mercenaries, activists mooning the WTO, your stockbroker, a favorite cast member on *Survivor* —as long as you wait for the signal from the criers on the watchtowers of Commerce & Finance: *Five o'clock, and all is well!*

Janus, god of theory, can tell us whether, from one minute to the next, we're on a losing side or a winning side. While the market puts stock in nothing but the measure of the moment, Janus can, at will, peer into the past and divine the future. Will tomorrow be different? And will it be new, too? Oh, yes, it will be very fresh, with sunrise in the East and sunset in the West, simultaneously ending and beginning all day long, and no smart aleck asking how long it'll last (now is enough) and no cynic accusing some marketing department of buying a month-to-month lease on Janus' voice (Janus never speaks while the Fortune 500 are drinking water).

Janus cannot be trusted, as no thinker can be trusted (no thinker asks to be trusted, only taken seriously), for the war has already happened while so many wars are still happening, and a god, like a theory, can only be rich in acolytes. Shiny words amuse, and soft ones comfort, and if you are intelligent, you will feel stymied by what the world has been and is and likely will be. You will feel the weight of enlightenment on your brow, and it will make you sleep, perhaps to dream, but rarely to switch phone companies, let alone to quit your job in protest.

EXPLICATIVE ITERATION OF THE PREVIOUS § JANUS, GOD OF THEORY. There exists the human tendency to theorize and concoct rules of cause and effect, to generalize from experience, to abstract from the anecdote, incidentally one of our greatest strengths, this capacity granting us perspective and thus the power to overcome the superstition of local coincidence and apprehend the world in proportion. This same human capacity for abstraction and generalization can also be put to more devious uses by those in whose interest it is to do so, e.g. business and government appropriating prognostications as reassuring distractions, firing off jargon-filled nonsense in order to invite critics to accept deference as inevitable. Witness the inexplicable degree of our deference to prognosticators like Alan Greenspan, Donald Rumsfeld, Bill Gates, and, well, hell, remember all the "experts" mooing blissfully during the bubble of the Nineties? Theories back then converged and were sung sweetly through our collective throat. It's an uncomplicated example of complacent herd mentality, and this danger haunts every context, economic, political, academic, and otherwise. Theories can be better than this, obviously, competing in the critical arenas of journals and conferences, opposing theories launched at each other in primitive dialectical showdowns like jury-rigged robots in those robo-battles you see on cable where victory is often circumstance-dependent. But the point is authority anywhere is susceptible to thinking too well of itself; and we, too well of it. And the troubling thing about *this*—the abdication of our skepticism in favor of knowing self-congratulation—is that *we know this & concede anyway*. So, anyway....

ANGELS OF MERCY. Are you lost? Or are you unwilling to admit cowardice in the muscle of your heart? When the economic calculations are made, weighing opportunistic careerism against good, ethical, soulful work, you are a prophet: you know which way your scales will tip. Ah, well. Self-preservation is an instinct of the apes whose genetic hides we have not fully shrugged off. Life advances not on the moving sidewalks of theoretical strategies, but on the messy improvisations of the vine-to-vine swing that we call a case-by-case basis. Maybe an easier crisis will come your way, one in which hypocrisy will feel as natural as a wool sweater and a judgment call will have nothing more at stake than money. Mortals can always try again (up to a point). In the meantime, be a patriot. Go shopping. Behold the wings of angels at the mall. In the feathers of sales tags will you find the map of your destiny revealed. It will have a magnetic strip on it.

MERLIN'S EYE. Might this secret off-hours work be, in practical consequence, a kind of free R&D for our corporate masters? Rather than pay for the next cool big hot fast sweet thing, they hire a snoop to watch the monitors, peeping for promise, salivating for talent to hire or product to swipe. This risk—that your love's labor might become a love's labor lost—is one you must accept, while guarding, as best you can, the ramparts of your intellectual property from the dark magic of Merlin's lawyers (and the brainless apprentice copying and pasting your online portfolio). It's a risk all creative workers assume. The economic risk is less unnerving than the haunting prospect that even your secret work is susceptible to appropriation by the very forces from whom you have, supposedly, hidden yourself.[3]

SOLITUDE. Doing secret off-hours work doesn't mean you work alone. An untried neophyte, I've offered to do work for little to no *dinero* to build my chops, attack with purpose, sting like I mean it. I've done posters for bands, book covers for small presses, brochures for my mother's business, flyers for bars, whatever for whomever. This is my school, and I'm the only one in the classroom. More importantly, while it's "for real," it's as close to unpaid as a penny on the lip of a sewer—which means my benefactors shouldn't look my gift pony in the mouth. But they do, you know they do. Here is an observation: doing free work for people deprives them of the means to appreciate the value of what you've done. Danger, danger. So, okay, maybe sometimes I choose to work alone, sulking like a philosopher, a lonely cowboy of wisdom, a blade of straw set in the grim corner of my mouth. Yes, sometimes doing free work on behalf of clients who can't afford top-notch pro chops earns me a feather of goodwill today and paying work tomorrow. Against all odds and the flinty nature of the human brain, this happens. All other times, in fraternity with the designer down the street and for the greater social good, I charge.

VICARIOUS EXPERIENCE. Speaking of the greater social good, I suspect we are bored by the nostrum that art has

no social utility; it has meaning and, occasionally, consequence. While it won't mow the lawn, it will allow us to
experience the world from the perspective of the teenager
mowing it. Graphic design might depict any of this: the
mower, the manufacturer, the grass, the fertilizer, the
teenager, the digital audio player, the homeowners, the
lurking landscapers, the suburb, the gas station, the city
planners, the county, the state of nature, the world of apathy. In choosing perspective and defining a worldview, you
must make critical judgments. If you choose one perspective, you are rejecting all others. On what basis? According
to what principles? On whose behalf? To what end?

Read a novel, and you will experience the world from
another's point of view. This vicarious experience makes
for excitement and enlightenment, sympathy and empathy, diversion and compassion, all of which can be counted
soundly on the side of Social Goods. Literature's instrumental benefits (what readers get out of it) are not what
motivate authors to create. Authors tend to resort to
hyperbole and analogy to describe their inspiration: they
give birth, channel gods, set planets in orbit. They are
moved by mysterious forces, possessed by muses, driven
by demons. Nevertheless, authors must also make critical
judgments: *from whose point of view will I write, and whose
story will I tell?* Once made, these decisions require commitment. That's why it's so critical for these decisions to
be fueled by passion and piloted by good judgment—or else
the rocket, failing escape velocity, will tumble to Earth.

Artists and writers are not immune to the desire to
please and are not above pandering, preaching and selling
out. The boundary between artists and designers—artists
build sand castles while designers surrender to the under-

tow of business—has never been clear; in fact, the spectrum is well served by the beach analogy in that one never can be sure where the beach ends and the ocean begins. Artists are commissioned; novelists are hired to ghost-write autobiographies of industry leaders; and Cassandre originals fetch sums envious to fine artists toiling away in factory lofts. Not to mention that an artist and designer are often one and the same person, the transformations accomplished with nothing more epic than the skirt-hoisting updraft of a financial transaction (= **DESIGNER**) or the sleeve-rolling hunker-down of a Saturday at home (= **ARTIST**). The critical judgment of a graphic designer, therefore, may be helpfully considered to be analogous to that of an artist or author. One peculiar hazard for graphic designers, however, is that by appropriating a worldview, they might, by means of that commercial appropriation, unfang the critique contained within it. It is a risk artists and authors, perhaps to their detriment, don't worry about as instinctively as designers.

Designers, on the other hand, cannot let themselves off the hook by claiming the powers and refusing the responsibilities, by saying *I'm as good as any artist* one day and *the client made me do this crap* the next. You have to put your choices where your cursors are. Choices define you: your priorities, loyalties, hopes. Abstention is impossible. You must make judgments. Where does curiosity hold your eye? Whose perspective do you want your audience to vicariously experience, and why? What story do you want to tell?

Notice I didn't say "what story *should* be told" or "what story *hasn't yet* been told." I said, "What story do YOU WANT to tell?" The "you" and the "want" are key words here, emphasizing your personality and desire, rather than (a) ethical obligation, (b) a duty to compensate for gaps in the social narrative, or (c) a commitment to the client that trumps all else (that's an excuse for a failure of imagination). We're talking about *desire* desire, not whim, fancy, impulse or preference—we're talking guts and grit, who you love, why you fight, how you live your life, not what color shirt goes with sullen denial. If you lack passion for your work, if all you have to run in are someone else's floppy clown shoes, then it will show in your sorry performance. Better to stumble on your own than finish an indentured third.

Better to fail in your work than to work for your failure.

CLARIFICATION RE: THE STORY. I should clarify that I am not suggesting the story you want to tell is your own. Like writers imagining themselves in the positions of their characters, inhabiting their points of view to best describe their experiences, designers can choose to see and thus depict the world from the POV of just about anyone and anything, from an endangered ocelot to the Army Corps of Engineers, from an abused spouse to a CEO. It makes a difference whether you choose to experience the construction of roads and boat ramps near the Rio Grande River from the POV of the displaced ocelots or the hardworking Army Corps of Engineers; or whether you choose to experience the divorce proceedings from the POV of the abused and disabled husband or the CEO who worked twenty years while her husband raised the kids. These are not simple stories and they are not your stories, but your work is to find POV entries into these stories that inspire you. An intense and fully felt perspective will inform your book, poster, illustration, website . . . .

CLARIFICATION RE: THE NATURE OF DESIRE. That I am writing—and can't stop writing—this essay I find curious—or, perhaps, emblematic. I never once said, "I want to write an essay about graphic design." The way I've talked about desire, though, would lead one to presume that I believe that that's what happens, that one scouts the terrain, flag in hand, and announces, "I want that hill." That scenario can be distracting because it calls to mind the phrase "force of will," a phrase that implies you are forcing yourself to do something because you feel the pull of an obligation or the push of coercion. The desire I'm talking about—and the kind of will that is powered by desire and makes real what was once imagined—is much different in that it has to do with the expression of one's personality. Where does desire come from? Where does it start? What are its origins? It comes. It starts. It originates. But the words come later, if only moments later, as a description of what one felt. Only after the gut rumbles does the mind name its appetite.

DESIGNER AS ACTOR. Designers are like actors. They take on roles written by others. They take direction. They try to keep in mind the performances of those, if any, who have played the roles before them. While trying to satisfy the director, the writer, and tradition, actors/designers try to make the roles their own. This may be why designers rarely hold strong beliefs. They are actors and assume the beliefs of others. They identify with the wants and fears of someone else, even someone as imaginary as a typical consumer or a reasonable person. But maybe one shouldn't fault designers for the circumstances in which they work. We are all pressured by circumstance, by the demands of those above us and the needs of those close to us, by the heat of the lights, by the edge of the stage beyond which we tumble into the orchestra pit. We all inhabit characters depending on where we find ourselves—the office, the mall, the shower, the courtroom—and obey, to greater and lesser extents, the social and cultural conventions inherent in these places. Still, we must all negotiate our unique compromises that enable us to move through these spaces, that enable us by the abrasions of our personalities to make our marks† on the walls, or by our stubbornness to knock them down. Unlike the citizen called to court or the student to the front of the class, designers can choose whether or not to audition, whether or not to take the role, and whether or not to change the script. Like the power of the actor, the power of the designer is exercised in the series of judgments that must be made. These judgments compose the creative space in which the designer acts. The designer's art consists in how the designer makes these judgments, and what these judgments are.

PERILOUS FIGHT. Graphic designers are as vulnerable as lawyers and writers to the temptation to overidentify with their clients. *Over*identify. Lawyers argue their clients' cases as if "zealous representation" were merely the first stage in a spiritual transference, in which a balding forty-year-old defense attorney is possessed by the assumptions and slang of a twenty-six-year-old pro quarterback from Memphis. Hired to fire off news releases, ad copy, and annual reports, writers employed in the communications

---

† Middle French *designer*, to designate, from Medieval Latin *designare*, from Latin, to mark out, from *de-* + *signare*, to mark.

and public-relations departments of institutions from auto companies to zoological societies clothe their minds in the worldviews of their employers as if slipping into something a little more comfortable. And graphic designers, suspended like an electric current in the gelatin between client and target market, endure a stress no different in nature and succumb to overidentification no different in degree.

WARNING:

OVERIDENTIFICATION MAY CAUSE MYOPIA, STIFFNESS, STUPIDITY, INTOLERANCE, ARROGANCE, AND DEBILITATING CO-DEPENDENCY.

On behalf of the client, the lawyer communicates to the jury; the writer, to readers; the designer, to an audience. This is going to sound crazy, but consider Jesus. Mediating between God and Man stands Jesus, speaking in parables that must be interpreted, telling stories that signify deeper meanings the way chop in the water implies rocks, wind and current. And, like Jesus, lawyers, writers and graphic designers (and lots of other folks, too) shoulder a dilemma of identification: how to balance the role of emissary with the role of savior, the fact of servitude with the dream of redemption. We designers can always excuse ourselves by appealing to the temporary nature of our assignments, the urgency of paying today's bills, the necessity of commercial relationships, and the possibility of mutual benefit. If it's good enough for Jesus to die, come back, and live to work another day, then it's good enough for us, too.

Yes, well, you're no Son of Mary. Jesus had something to say, and the Big Guy ain't whistling in *your* ear. You're on your own, stuck in the middle of you. What parables can you come up with, and will they have more meat on their bones than the morsel of one interpretation? If you're not feeling the Jesus example, then go Nietzsche.

What is needed, to paraphrase Friedrich, is style.[4] Personal style. Moral style. Outfit your bad self by developing your desires, values, and goals. The lifelong process of challenging convictions to forge new ones revitalizes your imagination. And to hell with a balanced life and a moral compass pointing north to Convention. Work so hard you make yourself sick. Nietzsche did. And Jesus never ate soy burgers, ran on a treadmill, or stayed out of the sun. A balanced life may suffice as a subject for a lifestyle magazine, but if the magazine is laid out well, you can bet the designer is an imbalanced hellcat.

WARNING:
OVERIDENTIFICATION MAY CAUSE EMBARRASSING GESTURES IN CROWDED ROOMS, EXISTENTIAL PANIC AT HOME, AND LOSS OF VISION.

Overidentifying with a client means you will sacrifice your poise to defend your client's case. You will crouch at midnight in the pall of your refrigerator light and wonder who more than a hollow shell you are. At meetings, you will hear words flying out of your mouth like magician's doves, and you will vaguely recall that, once upon a time, you thought for yourself. Overidentifying with a client means you'll conceal yourself within one perspective and cut a single eye-hole in the cardboard box you believe is a hat. You will not be proud of the work you produce in this manner.

Overidentification = loss of self but also forfeiture of
that singular creativity for which, whether they know it
or not, your clients are paying. To continually solicit and
defer to what your clients think they want is lazy, cheap,
and disrespectful. You should try to give them what you
would want if you were in their positions—and still you.

To guard against the perils of overidentification, designers must develop a strong sense of self, alarmed with a
healthy skepticism triggered by the motives of anyone
seeking to buy your brain and grope your person.

THE BOON OF LIMITATION. Working on a project for a client
limits the choices available, especially when compared
with sitting down to a blank page or blank screen at home
on the weekend. Freedom (when defined as the absence
of unreasonable obstacles and the presence of meaningful
choices) leaves a vacuum in which the imagination is
sucked thin, dispersed like gas molecules obedient to the
entropy of space. Limitations focus the mind like gravity.
They narrow the field of possibility by eliminating choices.
Still, you need a presence of mind to steer through the
absence of guidance. You must opt as well as discard; you
must eventually, after *NO*, say *YES*. Working for a client
delivers a sensation of relief by eliminating choices for
you, whereas on your own you have to reject and select
according to your own lights. Solo, you become your own
client and, at times, your own audience, much like writers
admit they write for no audience but themselves.
Independence is hard work, and the labor will strengthen
your constitution, developing not only the way in which
you work but the person you are becoming. These processes
—working for a client and working for yourself—are relat-

ed and have much in common, but you can guess that working for yourself will galvanize your character from the heart outward, an experience akin to being dropped in a jungle and, with nothing more than boots and a haircut, finding your way home.

INSPIRATION & SELF-CONSCIOUSNESS. Inspiration is tricky. You work what you feel. The mind leaps to visions of the finished product before you've figured out how to get there, and you don't know whether it's worth getting there. Self-consciousness hits early in the process, lighting firecracker questions under your office chair, making it nearly impossible to concentrate, to even *start*.

Is this my best? Is it even good enough? What will the client think? What will the audience think? Will they laugh? Will they laugh because my design stinks or because they think that I can't see that my design stinks? They might forgive me if they think I'm in a hurry, cranking these things out every hour. But maybe they think I don't care enough about the job. Maybe they think I don't care enough about them. Maybe they resent my apathy. Maybe they have only contempt for my innocence.

And this is during the thinking phase, before you've done a damn thing, what with every cat of an idea scared back out the window by the firecracker pops of self-doubt. Self-consciousness can be the *saboteur* of inspiration. You audition ideas and reject them, one after the other, for any number of criteria, some valid, some based only in fear of humiliation. If you're scared by what people will think, for example, because you've revealed too much, been too honest or personally forthcoming, then maybe the most worthwhile and moving work you've done is also the work you're most likely to reject, and for the wrong reasons. Previewing your work to someone else often confirms your fears. Sometimes you just have to risk it.

Your design sensibility will never develop if you aren't conscious of these criteria. Reliance on intuition is a cop-out, a euphemism for whim or caprice, an easy way to get into trouble. Defining your criteria is critical so that you can, later, determine whether adherence to these criteria helped you or hurt you. If you don't ask yourself why you rejected that idea and selected this one, you will either (a) take all credit for your successes and blame others for your failures, in which case you will be an asshole, or (b) greet every day with the nauseous suspicion that it will be your last, in which case you will be pitiful.

You may never establish your true criteria. Or, to be more accurate, you may never establish the way in which your mind midwifed your idea; you may never be conscious of exactly how and why your brain processed discrete bits of data and memory, layered them with associations and daydreams, suppressed instinct, snapped fear from a synapse, flung love in the sulci. (If you could be conscious of precisely all elements of this process and if you could control all of it, wouldn't we all just *choose* to alter the process until we were superior designers, and therefore wouldn't we all *be* superior designers?[5]) It is after the operation of this creative process that you return to your memory, as it were, of the scene of the crime. You attempt, by asking questions, to discern what criteria might best define the judgments you actually made. You didn't like this one design you imagined and you rejected it; why? You chose this other design idea, and, working it out, you feel it still doesn't look right; why not? The criteria might fit only awkwardly, a glass slipper for the wrong daughter, and so there is much trial and error. But the trying on of criteria is necessary to determine your criteria, to birth them into the light, and to be conscious not so much of how well you satisfied them in the past but, instead, of how wisely you might deploy them tomorrow *even within this same design*. Criteria function as summary judgments of the past. They are the mental tools with which you guide the redesign of your design.

DISSENT. In dissent, someone might point out that criteria already exist; designers throughout history have been defining and naming them, employing them and discussing their efficacy. In reply, I would argue that these criteria, too, are judgments of another past, codifications of the observations of successful and failed experiments through-out the history of art and design. And while designers may rediscover these criteria, defining the operations of their own creative imaginations in similar terms, that doesn't mean the self-consciousness of a designer's experience is any less personal. Because consciousness in general exists doesn't mean that I experience self-consciousness in a general way. Likewise, I experience the process of discov-ering and defining my working criteria as painfully particular. I am predated but not preempted by others.

MORAL CONTENT. The moral content of work: it's all dandy to WANT and to KNOW and to WORK, but these vessels may be as likely filled with toxic sludge as fruit smoothie. A designer may want very badly to promote neo-Nazism among rural schoolchildren or mail anthrax to the cast members of *The Hughleys*. The desire to work is not the final answer.

> . . . Art thou afeard
> To be the same in thine own act and valour,
> As thou art in desire?

> Said Lady Macbeth, *Macbeth*, Act I, Scene 7.

Designers are no one special. Like everyone a-rafting on the river of American Commerce, they must work with reference to The Good (see Plato, et al[6]), and not just ethical goodness (a weighing of social benefits) but also moral goodness (a judgment call on right and wrong). So you want to be a designer? Self-definition through work creates a personality, develops the flesh-and-mind hybrid that is you, the you that strives and grieves, mourns the departure of your lover and rails against the spread of political apathy, and it is this personality that now has purchase in the world.[7] Ever vigilant to protect the moral content of your design process against virulent ideologies and dogmatic infections, you must also be ever ready to deploy the powers of citizenship on behalf of what is good for you, best for society, and right for humanity.

"The only thing I can recommend at this stage," said then-President Vaclav Havel in a speech in Budapest in 1999, "is a sense of humor, an ability to see things in their ridiculous and absurd dimensions, to laugh at others and at ourselves, a sense of irony regarding everything that calls out for parody in this world. In other words, I can only recommend perspective and distance . . . A good mind . . . Vigilance of spirit."[8]

THE GOOD MIND. A good mind depends upon the capacity to think coherently and not the habit to worship the image.[†] A good mind contains respect for fact and empathy for people, distrust of authority and the courage to argue. A good mind is vigilant against abuses of power, the signs of corruption, the wages of deceit and the wizard behind the curtain. A good mind delights in the joys of discovery, the unscripted conclusions of experiment. A good mind values history, not myth; import, not ideology; narrative, not montage; argument, not superstition; character, not stereotype; and language, not icon. All this may mean that we are asking of ourselves as designers what we ask of our writers, artists, lawyers, and, most broadly, all of us as active citizens: to think, speak, and argue as if we mattered.

WORD VS. IMAGE. This emphasis on argument, narrative and language would seem to betray the bias of the writer and lawyer I am. But more so, I think (perhaps defensively) that this emphasis is predetermined when the designer's frustration is with the inadequacy of image as substitution for the complex nature of genuine thought. Narrative in literature has been deconstructed to reveal the artificiality of linear composition as well as the posturings of authority. But image is no automatic improvement when the goal is to strip away falsehood, deception, and posturing to honor honesty, ambiguity, and ambivalence. As media theorists[††] have been murmuring since the spread of television and hollering since the Vietnam war, the image, as produced and consumed, is even better suited to achieve the devious ends to which iconography is aimed.

---

† *Iconolatry* is the worship of icons or images.
†† Please don't make me quote Marshall McLuhan.

Today the visual dominates, and it seems as if image and icon have usurped the role of narrative and argument. It is against this usurpation of discourse that I sling my critical stones. Does this simply mean graphic designers should use more text?

WORDS IN A FRAME. The problem with relying on text to convey genuine argument is that the designer still has to contend with the commercial context, with the fact that a message of, say, abstinence is delivered by a porn star. Here, for grins, is text from a recent Audi print ad: "The rules are what you make them. These four leaders [9] prove it. By following passion, not convention, they make the world a bigger place than we thought it was. At Audi, we know greatness doesn't come from following rules, but from believing in possibilities. Never quit. Never do the expected. Never rest on your laurels. Never think great is good enough. NEVER FOLLOW."

First after reading this I think, *What total bullshit.* There's an old Steve Martin bit where he gets the audience to repeat, after him, the promises contained in the Nonconformist's Oath ("I promise to be unique," etc.), and when Steve, finally, yells out, "I promise not to repeat things other people say," a whole stadium of people responds with only a weak syllable or two ("I pro . . . mise") before the air is sucked out of their lungs, the joke dawns on them, and in embarrassment, they grant Steve the acknowledgment of a low murmur of laughter, and Steve, quickly, moves on to the next bit.[10] So, okay, there's this irony that arises out of the conflict between content and context, and it's one where context wins, putting our human gullibility right in our face, and so we laugh politely

in an unstated but very much understood mutual agree-
ment to forgive and forget the rude cleverness of Mr.
Comedian as long as we can all, as a society, *move on*.

Second thing I think is can you imagine management
posting this boastful Never Follow ad in the hallway beside
the zero-tolerance sexual-harassment posters and the
calendar for that month's team meetings? "At Audi, we
know greatness doesn't come from following rules." They
may say they know it, but I'm sure they don't believe it.
I mean, *never* follow? These are *German auto engineers*,
after all.

Third thing I think after reading the Audi ad is *Christ,
this is the kind of language* I *use*. Yes, it's expressed in the
shorthand sloganeering of those Successories posters, but
"passion, not convention" and "possibilities" not "rules"
and "never follow," I mean, shit, this language is trashed
of meaning by the dynamic whereby (a) I know this is an
ad trying to flatter my independent spirit and thus sell me
a car with which I will associate this independent spirit but
(b) I also know the ad folks must understand that someone
truly independent and intelligent is going to recognize this
ad for the b.s. it is but (c) then also be capable of differen-
tiating between the ad as b.s. and the ad as well-honed
message for a very specific audience which (d) can't really
be a dopey group of soft-thinking suckers likely to be sincerely flattered by the patronizing notion that consumer
obedience = personal independence, which is what the
intelligent independents would like to believe (that the
target market consists of suckers who are very much *not
them*), because, after all, (e) the target audience is a demographic rich enough to buy expensive German luxury/sport
automobiles for chrissakes and therefore must be doctors,

lawyers, professionals, and businesspeople, most of whom
are not the types one thinks of as dopey and soft-thinking,
and so (f) the intelligent independents must accomplish
a kind of self-dissociation from their immediate reading-
this-ad circumstance in order to understand the ad's
message as patronizing b.s. intended for wealthy suckers
not them and so (g) by excising themselves from the ad's
demographic, they achieve a maneuver in which they also
excise themselves subjectively from this ad-reading circumstance so that this whole dynamic is something that
happens to *other people* and not them and so now, safe and
superior, they can look on as amused spectators, a remove
which, ironically, allows them the luxury of (h) *enjoying
this ad*. This is pretty much exactly what I do when I listen
to the Steve Martin tape wherein he gets the audience to
repeat his Nonconformist's Oath: I excise myself from the
experience and become a supraspectator laughing at the
joke on the audience in the safe knowledge that the joke
is not on me because *I am not a member of the duped
audience*.

These complex mental maneuvers we engage in to protect our egos enable the ad's message, eventually, to reach
us because we believe we have made ourselves unreachable and so what's the harm in letting our guards down
now that we know we're not the target? And the irony on
irony is that once we've done this, let in this ad's message,
have we suddenly let ourselves become what we dreaded
most: duped suckers? And so now we *are* the ad's intended
market? And is this whole dynamic what allows us to move
sanity-intact through the ad-saturated world in a kind of
self-insularity, a mental force-field that while protecting
our feelings lets in through its permeable membrane the

very messages we want to believe we aren't receiving?

Now we come to my distaste for Audi co-opting the language of independent thinking: the people who use this language and respond to it are now less likely to use it and respond to it because they have this icky feeling toward it, a distrust for being conned by it somehow. It has degenerated into the language of con artists. This distrust extends beyond the commercial context and into daily life and culture, wherein I might wisecrack to a buddy, "You sound like an Audi commercial," and, wham, I've destroyed the power and sincerity of his language and the only thing for me and my buddy to do now is *to move on*—and hope to share a chummy laugh when we hear the same exchange during an episode of *The Simpsons*.

With language thus emptied and made vacuous, I as a designer find myself in a very unhappy locked-in situation in which I can't trust my words on the page because I don't even trust the language in my head. It's enough to ground the air force of your imagination when you consider that even when you cobble together a new vernacular of your own, that language may also soon enough be repurposed in a new context, wrung dry of meaning, and reduced to a quip on an animated sitcom. The remedy we all seem to accept, which is not so much a remedy, is to just keep working in willful ignorance or else big dumb hope, landing the blows of language on the mug of an inflatable clown that will never stop coming up for more.

LIES. The designer's presumed duty is to conspire with the client in concealing truth, hiding facts, and dismissing as irrelevant and old-fashioned the insistence on the scientific method and the capacity for receiving any and all

news from the world whatever its instrumental value for
or against the selling of product and service. Facts undermine salesmanship. Reality holds no powers in the realm
of marketing. Argument enjoys no champions at point-
of-sale kiosks. Polls and market research are means of fer-
reting out obstacles and streamlining the infusion of myth
by way of the needles of image and icon. Designers are
liars. We are complicit with trickery. Like campaign consultants, publicists, and cosmetic surgeons, we are
proficient in gloss, skew, tuck and shine. We may be
employed to defuse resistance or minimize damage, but
if by smoke and cleavage we are unable to preserve the
audience's credulity in the magician's voodoo, then we
are unlikely to be rehired.

EXCEPTIONS. Designers in academia and scientific insti-
tutes as well as loyalists to the work of Edward Tufte may
take uproarious umbrage at the accusation that they are
liars, complicit in deceit. But indignation begs the question. The designer is not the one generating the statistics;
is unlikely to be in a good position to challenge the numbers; and is often beholden to the parameters set by the
institutions that want to use these tables, charts, dia-
grams, and graphs in persuading others to fund their
projects, side with their causes, or support their policies.
It is certainly old news to learn statistics can be manipulated, and for decades critical academics have been
defining the inherent biases of statistical analysis and
devising ways to minimize their effects. Self-policing and
self-criticism exist to greater and lesser extents in most
sciences, and integrity abounds in all professions, to be
sure. As a lawyer and writer of fiction, I include myself

squarely in the camp of those who must struggle between the primacy of fact and the allure of imagination, between observation of our objective world and expression of our emotional lives. It is not oceanography, standard deviation, or the Krebs Cycle that I am questioning. It is the essence of the job of the designer that I seek to complicate by teasing out its contradictions and tensions. Lies can be pretty, they can obscure and distract, they can maintain decorum during a family reunion in which uttered truth could cause a hundred wills to be rewritten. The fact is that no profession can resist temptation in all its guises. *We are not safe from ourselves.*

HALF-OFF CLEARANCE, ALL TRUTH MUST GO. Any relationship a designer has with the truth is complicated by the commercial context in which the designer's work is used and disseminated. It is a truth almost universally acknowledged that a seller in possession of a well-designed product must be in pursuit of a consumer. The seller may prosecute that pursuit by virtually any message necessary, and the seller knows the market can accommodate messages of almost any hue and deviance, including those messages of anti-consumerism and pro-individualism but especially those that encourage consumers to dream an impossible dream that has nothing whatever to do with the product itself and works mainly by means of conditioned association. Whether a particular advertising or marketing campaign succeeds or fails in service of its particular product, it will always succeed by contributing its share toward the larger goal of all advertising and marketing, which is to promote the legitimacy of shopping itself as the primary way of engaging the world.

Producers of goods are subject to standards of quality and safety, held to warranties, and answerable to consumer complaints and product-liability lawsuits. Messages contained in the advertising and marketing (and thereby graphic design) related to the product have to adhere to certain guidelines and restrictions (as everything must)—restrictions on obscenity, unsubstantiated claims, slander, revealing trade secrets of competitors, etc.—but as anyone who has been alive for the past thirty years can attest, it certainly feels like advertisers can do and say pretty much whatever the heck they want. The findings of *Consumer Reports* notwithstanding, an advertiser can claim that their product is the best, number one, America's favorite, the world's choice, premier, top notch, unparalleled, unbeaten, unbeatable, incomparable, the ultimate, the genuine preference of sitcom actors under thirty, the greatest, the purest, the smoothest, the hottest, the most asked-for on Mars, Pluto and Uranus. Elegant colors, snappy type, and sexy packaging deceive by flattery: *if you want something this cool, then you must be cool, too.*

Advertisers, it seems, can also say whatever the heck they want pretty much *wherever* the heck they want. There are different rules for broadcast advertising than for print advertising, and federal and state governments can restrict advertisements for tobacco, drugs, liquor, firearms, gambling, and pornography. There are restrictions on advertising on public property, like in government buildings, libraries, and schools, but fast-food chains and soft-drink companies now have limited access to those very cafeterias and hallways once off-limits.[11] The way consumerism has insinuated itself into nearly every pore of the skin of our world exhausts one's capacity for documentation. You could spend three lives cataloging the features of this complexion: product placements in movies and television, graphics painted on buses and stadiums, logos stitched on our hats and shoes, jingles playing on our computers and cell phones, banners on diapers and portable toilets.[12] We are so accustomed to its growing prevalence that to call attention to it is to call attention to oneself as an annoying and sheltered crybaby.[13]

That's the way it is. Suck it up. We all need to make a living.

For the purposes of graphic design, this state of commercial affairs is a given. When designing, you know your design is not only competing for the approval of your client; it's competing for attention in a race millions have entered. You're likely to try anything, however extreme or odd, to be noticed. Your design is one single runner in the Boston Marathon of the marketplace. Good luck.

Given this saturated world of commercial messages, the ubiquity of deception, the bias for the extreme,[†] and the

---

† I feel like I've caught myself in a contradiction here, on the one hand accusing most ads/designs of being timidly conservative and on the other identifying a bias for the extreme. I think I can resolve it by arguing that most ads cautiously play to the consumer's presumed thin-skinned expectations, which is exactly the context above which other advertisers/designers resolve to rise by resorting to extreme tactics, whether sexual, "controversial," annoying, or tasteless in nature. If you want to be noticed, how do you do it? Is a great design enough? Or do you have to be annoying, salacious, rude, or scatalogical? And, more to the point, just because your design/ad is noticeable or has been noticed (by consumers or the media), it isn't true that any notice is good notice. People may notice your ugly stupid potty-joke of an ad and stay the hell away. Companies after all don't want consumers to talk among themselves; they want consumers to buy their shit.

apathy of the consumer, what should a designer's relationship with the truth be?

SHOW SOME RESPECT. Acknowledging the reality of the designer's current role, it seems downright unfair to expect a measure of truth-telling or—imagine this—to insist on truth as a standard when judging designs (how thick would the *Print* Annual be then?). Truth—so goes the feeling—ain't the game we're playing. Asking a designer for a measure of commitment to the truth is like asking a baseball player, "Yes, but how well can you *kick* the ball?"

Thus we live with lies of all kinds, hoping that most are benign and that, in the long run, the insidious lies confer more benefits than they exact costs. We prefer to believe that partial truths, half truths and nothing but the untruths add to the entertainment value of salesmanship. And just in case, we also like to believe that it is enough to leave the burden of discrimination on government agencies enforcing the rules and consumers withholding their dollars and banishing the weak.[14] Yes, gone are the days of Dr. Crock's Cure-All Elixir, and, while it's true that today we are more cynical and understand that less (truth) is more (exciting), enough of us still manage to keep the phone lines busy for the latest fads in diet, exercise, self-help, and chatting with the dead.[15]

All of this is not to argue for a rigid standard of truth—whether journalistic, legal, or scientific—as the next controversial duty in the designer's code. Not every designer can work for public-interest law firms, watchdog groups, the National Institute of Health, the Smithsonian, and the *New York Times*, not to mention that working for an organization whose mission statement pairs "commitment" and "truth" in the same sentence is not the same as committing *yourself* to a pursuit of the truth (even righteous organizations may ask you as a designer to please know your place and remember in whose stewardship the pursuit of truth resides).

But when a *respect* for truth is met with sniggering or a rolling of the eyes, when it feels so antiquated, out of touch, unrealistic, naïve, unfair, and downright silly, you have to take stock of your role as a designer and wonder how much sense it makes to feel this ambivalent, complacent, powerless, and used in your job. Personally, I don't share this cavalier disregard for the truth, and I believe there must be a place for it outside of the lip service paid to it in anti-smoking PSAs and episodes of *CSI*.

A designer's relationship to the truth is a fickle one based on opportunism, hypocrisy and acquiescence. Graphic designers, after all, owe their very existence to the market —to businesses and their need to sell, which makes businesses dependent on creative types for advertising, design, marketing, packaging, etc. Designers may have different thresholds of tolerance, but unless the message is obviously evil, misogynistic, racist, or perverted (video games, music and movies being the exceptions), we do what we gotta do.

It is possible, however, that respect for the truth is like our desire for self-expression. Truth is what we can get away with.[†] Treating it like any commodity, we trade it at our peril in the market, but truth does have a market. Like

---

† "Art is what you can get away with," said Andy Warhol. I'm not concerned with pulling a fast one on the audience, but asserting one's self against the impositions of authority.

genuine self-expression,[†] truth demands the risk of independence.

> "Enlightenment is humanity's departure from its self-imposed immaturity. This immaturity is self-imposed when its cause is not lack of intelligence but failure of courage to think without someone else's guidance. Dare to know! That is the slogan of the Enlightenment."
>
> —Immanuel Kant, from his 1784 essay, "What Is Enlightenment?"[††]

A DIGRESSION, WITH APOLOGIES. I hesitate to say too much (but I guess I'm going to) about those old Benetton ads, the ones where the controversy was not about the content of the photojournalistic images but about the decision to incorporate them into an advertisement, using gritty realistic "true" photos of a dying AIDS patient or civil-war refugees to basically sell sweaters in giddy colors fit for Dr. Seuss characters. Was this truth or provocation? integrity or cynicism? a thoughtful juxtaposition or commercially motivated shock tactic?

---

† Self-expression should not be mistaken for autobiography or confession. You can express anyone's story; it's the choice about what to express and how to express it that is the prerogative of the *self* in self-expression. Self-expression means the individual determines the form and content of the expression. It does not require the subject of the expression to be the self.

†† There are many translations of Kant's famous first paragraph of his essay. I took this concise and sober translation from Jacques Barzun's *From Dawn to Decadence* (HarperCollins, 2000).

It seems to me, with the benefit of hindsight, that these ads could be admired for publishing photos even mass-media outlets might have been squeamish about publishing and squeamish for the same reason that companies might be squeamish about using them in ads: the risk of alienating an audience enough so that they turn the page or change the channel. But the ads were still inauthentic in the sense that the photo's message had as much to do with the product or company as breasts do with beer or breweries. (Consider that the big boys behind the glass are worried about Janet Jackson's exposed breast certainly no less and maybe more than a dead American soldier: whatever upsets an audience.[16]) The point of an ad was then and remains today to announce, with the liar's straight face, that *this* is the kind of company we are, the kind who does *these* kinds of ads. And a company back then (late Eighties, early Nineties) could also congratulate itself for being the kind that was aware that any message they put in an ad was going to be judged according to its commercial context and so they were going to exploit that awareness by wearing politics as a fashion statement and controversy as an accessory and aren't we slickly postmodern and brave for doing so? Like today's reality TV where the only thing that's real is that you're really watching TV, the only thing true about these kinds of ads is that they truly get your attention—and really don't know what to do with it.

Because doing anything with your attention is not the point. Even Tibor Kalman's famous photo-retouched images (black Queen Elizabeth, white Spike Lee) were using race to tease our easy acceptance of icons, not challenging the legitimacy of employing icons in the first place.

He could've swapped gender or hair color, given someone
a disability, made the healthy, sick and the sick, healthy,
the rich, poor and the poor, rich. (Someone today could
have serious fun fooling with portraits of the Bush Admin-
istration, unless *Mad Magazine* has already done so [that
I can imagine *Mad* might do so is to reiterate that yesterday's subversion is today's convention, which is what
makes the job of today's political caricaturist so difficult].)
Kalman wasn't saying anything about graphic design's
troubling relationship with iconography and myth, even
if he thought he was; he was (I suggest, again with the
benefit of hindsight) employing the same means to send
a refined message: *please pay even more attention to
iconography*.

Tibor Kalman, who died in 1999, edited Benetton's *Colors*
magazine after Benetton was already notorious for their
"controversial" ad campaign. Apparently, he insisted that
graphic designers under his wing do *pro bono* design work
for charitable or non-profit entities, which is, in my mind,
an explicit recognition on his part of the unique benefits of
independent work. *Pro bono* work is honorable in a giving-
back-to-the-community way, making real a conscientious
commitment to social responsibility, but it's also one way
to escape the *status quo* of sublimating every residual
artistic urge into the celibacy of commercial interest.
Artistic urges are messy, self-critical, ambivalent; commercial interests are clean, simple, singular. And while you
might argue the tax status of an institution doesn't alter
the designer/client dynamic or soften the institution's
interest in self-preservation, I'd argue that, in practical
terms where the authority conceives of its nature and mission as charitable, altruistic, or political, it can and does.[17]

Most likely Kalman thought so, too. Most likely he believed that design was more than entertaining consumers and that designers now and then should risk making an argument that mattered to someone.[18]

Because as well-intentioned as a politically radical, charitably motivated designer is, he or she is almost always trapped in context. A provocative design when it's published commercially is like a wish the genie grants literally, leaving you rich and famous, yes, but you're Howard Hughes or Paris Hilton, not at all what you had in mind or in the least way asked for. Overlooking context is your downfall. Unless, of course, everyone politely ignores the context and, by the fiction of a social contract or professional courtesy, agrees to interpret your message like any other message, like journalism, art, a novel, or a critical essay, as if there were no way to distinguish among contexts, as if, in blatant disregard of the lessons of postmodern media theory, *the context didn't matter.*

I don't presume to suggest that an artist's obligation is to sabotage the tools of their trade, rip the canvas, renounce their medium. Also not suggesting that any message fails because it isn't self-critically masochistic enough (although, like art, it should be *in some measure* critical of its medium and itself). I'm struggling to come to terms with how tough it is to incorporate truth/argument/self-doubt/self-criticism/ambiguity/ambivalence into commercial graphic design without that incorporation itself neutering intent and defeating the purpose.

Design can obviously be successful without trying to do any of this. A design can simply be an ad that does a great straight-up job promoting a product, a brand, a company. That's the given. Also given is I'm not proposing that to improve the discipline you have to remove the *graphic* from graphic design. I am challenging the graphic, no doubt, the iconolatry, the easy way we have with mythologizing and sloganeering, the unquestioning serving up of the sweetly digestible comfort food of idealized symbol. The graphic designer in me enjoys this part of it, the creation of attractive things to look at. Love for making stuff is what pulled me in in the first place and keeps me there now. But the critic in me, especially the self-critic, the part of me that is both audience and skeptic, is unwilling to give design a free pass and is instead looking hard & thinking & *taking design seriously as art that demands to be interpreted*, and thus I consider the source, *the authority*, and the parameters that this authority enforced upon the creation, production and dissemination of the design. And I am frustrated and disappointed that so often, as a skeptical consumer and critical audience to whom these designs are aimed, I conclude, "Bullshit." And this *bullshit* is perfectly valid as the expression of my right as a consumer/critic to reject and sentence to disposability whatever commercial offering is before me. Whether out of consumer spite or in measured critical calculation, my rejection keeps my credit card in my pants and therefore must be accepted by the market. *Get thee gone.*

Maybe if I weren't so hard on design or on my goals for my own designs (someday), I could believe in what a recent Porsche ad asks me to believe in: "A simple turn of the ignition, and your faith in mankind is completely restored." Maybe if I just gave in, I'd be comforted by the hope that being taken for a ride will eventually get me somewhere.

THE MARKET FOR TRUTH. Any reevaluation of graphic design (its nature, standards and roles) depends on a review and critique of the market, the water in which the fish of graphic designers swim. When used sloppily as a catchall category (I indict myself among the guilty), "The Market" is subject to demonization one minute and lionization the next. The market is amoral and tends to reward the concentration of power, resulting in reduced competition and therefore market atrophy, and it is for its innate tendency to self-destruct that it's regulated. A regulated market breeds diversity, by which all of us are able to engage in this argument at all and expect the opportunity to put our theories into practice. Without a regulated market, designers would be laborers painting new lines in Wal-Mart parking lots and Going Out of Business signs in neighborhood downtowns. The market deserves criticism for many things, but it can also provide the opportunities for correcting its weaknesses.

The market as such is a far broader and looser concept than *consumerism*, which can be understood as a dark flowering growth in the great sprawling garden of the market. Technically, *consumerism* can refer to (a) the pro-consumer movement commonly associated with Ralph Nader's crusade for corporate responsibility in the form of safety standards, warranties, and honesty in advertising; (b) the theory that increasing consumption increases the social good; and (c) a kind of materialism in which all value is derived from the buying and using of consumer goods.[†] Consumerism[a|PRO] has much to recommend it: it

---

[†] Paraphrased from the definition of *consumerism* in *The American Heritage Dictionary, Third Edition.*

has improved the utility and ergonomics of products, the responsiveness of companies, and in general the operation of the market by increasing the quantity and quality of choices. Consumerism[b|THEORY] is pretty well acknowledged, its American and global implementations extensively criticized. Consumerism[c|VALUE] is what drives the application of Consumerism[b|THEORY], but it is clearly the weakest link in the chain, refutations abounding in the viciously addictive consumer cycle of desire » fulfillment » disappointment, its operation dependent not on its proof in the real world but on its hold in the minds of consumers.

We generally employ the term *consumerism* with the precision of a jack-knifing semi, sweeping all traffic conditions ahead of us with this blunt wedge of an implied criticism. Disillusion with Consumerism[c|VALUE] is generally the cause of this wrecking hostility, and it is a hostility that begins as self-disgust (for having bought into Consumerism[c|VALUE]) and is redirected outward toward the external correlative (Big Business) that perpetuates itself by exploiting the self-deluded consumer. Corporations are blamed for pandering to consumers with bland, manipulative, and lowest-common-denominator practices of product development, marketing, and advertising. Catering to consumers is what businesses do, the field of marketing itself being defined by its consumer-focus, and this hyperfocus, while positive in a Consumerism[a|PRO] way, can lead to shallow if not patronizing feedback loops in a negatively self-reinforcing Consumerism[c|VALUE] way. Once-burned-twice-spiteful critics argue that the unrelenting prevalence of messages of the Consumerism[c|VALUE] type numbs, deadens, and saddens us, locking us in an echo chamber of our own unfulfillable wishes, and that, in defense of ourselves as citizens and human beings, we mustn't forget that we can be taught, not just conditioned; we can learn, not just react; and that truth, while not a relevant subject in customer-satisfaction surveys, is a value to which we desperately need to grant its due.

Truth is inefficient, uneconomical, a hindrance, a cost of doing business, not a benefit of having done business, and it is only a grudging part of business at all because of Consumerism[a|PRO]. (Even in the world of journalism, the arduous search for truth is regarded as expensive, costly, at odds with the pursuit of profit.) As messengers of countervailing value systems, critics, artists, citizens, etc. need to employ their talents in forums at some remove from the influences of Consumerism[b|THEORY, c|VALUE]. The work of critical thought and artistic achievement is at its best antithetical (and anti-instrumental) to Consumerism[b|THEORY, c|VALUE] but in congruence with grander evaluations of human condition and aspiration.

Designers, like many, can do both. They can perform their functions as insiders, as client representatives, and they can marshal their private energies as outsiders, as friends of unwelcome truth and rude art. They can have their jobs—and their work, too.

And now we arrive again at the point wherein we soberly regard The Job for what it is and do not expect of it what it cannot deliver, and, needing what it cannot deliver badly enough to look for it outside The Job, we appeal to off-hours indie work for meaning & truth, for achieving excellence in a craft & transcendence in an art.

As independent workers—that is, as those working for one's self or for clients with few to no strings attached —designers may consciously avoid entanglements with

Consumerism[b|THEORY, c|VALUE] but may still work (risking failure on their own terms) within the broader context of The Market.

In criticizing one's role in the marketplace, the designer arrives at an ironic solution: *to participate more fully* in the marketplace—on the one hand, in the servant role; on the other, as a creator of content in one's own right. Designers harbor no antipathy for participating in the market *per se*, but they should have healthy skepticism for their pre-scribed roles within it (as acolytes of Consumerism[b|THEORY, c|VALUE]). Designers must understand the market well enough to be unwilling to settle for what's given and, instead, to find or create their own niches. The complacent take the path of least resistance and accept every meal the market serves. This is lazy gullible living and betrays a child's impatience for thought and a veteran's defensiveness for having already made, and contracted to lie in, the bed of a career. Designers are small fish in a big and turbulent sea, and the odds are always against the small fish. Still, this is no reason to surrender to any current that comes along. Surrender is not the work of a true believer; it's the path of the martyr.

Our regulated market (as opposed to consumerism) is based on the belief that the pursuit of self-interest is the best way to increase the social good (ensuring endless argument on whether or not empirical evidence supports the claim). In working on independent projects, designers may feel obligated to resist commercial pressures, to pursue their own self-interests (defined not as the accu-mulation of money but as something closer to the exercise of liberty), and to regard truth and excellence as values in themselves and not as means to ends or dead wood. If by pursuing desire, truth, independence, and excellence, designers find their ways back into existing markets or manage to create new markets for their work, that is surely one good (but not the only) way of identifying success.

SHOPPING & THE SELF, AN ASIDE. I would like someday to be as picky shopping for my jobs as I am shopping for my jeans and T-shirts. I feel so powerful as a consumer. *No. No. No.* It's intoxicating. Yes, as a buyer, I'm in a position of relative strength with respect to low-risk individual transactions, whereas when I'm a hopeful employee, I'm in a position of weakness as a seller of myself; clones of myself clutching résumés stretch in a line that weaves into the parking lot, or so it feels to me. It's the prerogative of the employer, now, to say to each of us candidates in succession, "No. No. No." Still, I'm fascinated by the fact that we are so quick to devalue ourselves as workers and take what's offered when at the same time, on the same day, we'll drive to five stores in five cities hunting for the best deal on a Toshiba DVD player. Oh, and the concept of returns! "I'd like to return my first year of employment, please, while it's still under warranty." "Was there anything wrong with your employment?" "Yes, Ma'am. It had several broken promises."

SUBVERTING MARKET CONVENTIONS (AS A MEANS OF RESISTING CONSCRIPTION INTO THE HARMED FORCES OF MINDLESS CONSUMERISM). What if, for the sake of argument, one wishes to buck the trend and design as a contrarian?

Consider the book designer who includes in the design a critique of the contents of the book by, for example, slugging the jacket with the blurb, "'This book sucks,' decries

Blip Foster, Graphic Designer." A breach of the designer's code, surely, and a good way to get fired, not to mention that, in this instance, the transgression can hardly mean very much to the graphic designer personally. Objecting to the contents of the book, the designer could decline the job. Don't do a cover for *Mein Kampf* or *Aryan Parades Throughout History* if you don't want to. If you simply didn't enjoy a particular book, found its premise thin, its characters shallow, then you'll probably hold your nose, retreat to a more generalized view of your place in the world of design (*my destiny lies elsewhere*), get the job done, and move on.

So, now, consider designing a cover for your own book (monograph, survey, essay collection, whatever). Even if you incorporate self-deprecating blurbs to undercut convention and advertise your ironic market-savvy sensibility, you still risk deterring even those buyers who get the joke. Even hipsters, unused to the practice of self-reliance, yield to the tyranny of What Is and entertain second thoughts. Picture the customer in the bookstore, wondering thus: *you know, maybe this book does suck; I know the book may be seducing me by flattering my discriminating intelligence; but maybe a book that says it sucks even if it's kidding is just another kind of book that actually sucks.* It's easier for the customer to exercise the feet and walk away than exercise the mind and think for oneself (or worse: having thought for oneself, the consumer unmasks you as a spiteful poseur who mocks the rules of the game because you can't play it). Rejection is the creator's recurrent nightmare, whether rejection by client, peer or audience, and this fear sobers designers real quick.

What is left for a contrarian to do? The fear of jeopardizing the market success of a book whose very subject is a critique of market values might be in most instances great enough to exhaust the most principled contrarian, forcing concessions of the kind (flattering blurbs, a precious author photo) that, later, induce self-disgust. If the book becomes a market success, the contrarian will likely be aroused by the flagrance with which self-disgust frolics in bed with self-admiration. The morning after, the contrarian harbors shameful doubts about his status as a contrarian, worries that this very market success, whose hair gel and thong he consented to wear, has ingested him and spit him back out, leaving of his once-coveted integrity nothing but a grin in a puddle, a pair of lips floating in the hypocrite he didn't think he had to be.

Subversion of market convention can, yes, be fun. In book and magazine design, for example, designers have played with the sizes and placements of titles, callouts, captions, the UPC, and all other standard features of the dull face, but play quickly devolves into empty tics, the way death comes for us all. Subversion is an old vehicle and, by itself, won't get you far before it backfires, stranding you road-side with singed hair, smoking clothes, and the question, *"Did I have anything I wanted to say in the first place?"* If all you had to say was that convention has nothing to say, well, you don't have much to say. Empty lashing out at the context of which you are a part reduces you to a teenager vandalizing the Geo your parents bought for you.

RISING CONFLATION. Possibly I have conflated market con-vention with design convention. Market convention can refer to many things, including agreed-upon norms of buy-ing and selling goods and services. New business models don't, by their novelty, subvert market conventions; they often reinforce them using new tools. Also, market convention influences design convention. For example, book-jacket blurbs are standard practice, but because their purpose is to persuade buyers, they are better understood as dictated by market convention rather than design convention. Subversion of convention in general (market, design, artistic, legal, or literary) is a beneficial and necessary activity, but in the long term, it makes for a hollow enterprise in that it can't sustain growth, either of itself (subversion becomes convention) or of the subverter (subverting one's own now-conventional subversion is the snake eating its tail).[19]

ENEMY OF TRANSCENDENCE. If frustrated designers long to make a statement that transcends the context in which it is made, they face a formidable foe in the funhouse mirrors of the marketplace: consumer advertising and corporate media distort the message of anyone walking its halls, making the serious appear goofy; the righteous, pathetic; and the dissenters, naïve as children, surprised by the goblins the mirrors make of their faces, and pouty that the world does not conform to their expectations. This is frustrating, to say the least, for graphic designers who wish to break the bonds of their given vernacular. Witness your self-consciously DIY design on a line of kids' T-shirts in Target, the chalk outline of your credibility marking the latest victim of context.[20]

Or even take a great ad, one that does something different, sporty, and catches your attention, and it does so squarely within the consumer context. The 216-page May 2004 issue of *Wired* falls open, as if by design, to a Mini

Cooper ad, the fat page elbowing its way front and center like a short guy with an inferiority complex who wants to be in the first row so the cameras can see him. The page is so thick because a sheet of stickers is glued to the back. The stickers are so-called "motoring callsign lettering," a maxi-moniker for what is a white script alphabet, one cap, two lower-case, A-Z, with, at the bottom, three stars and five lines of increasing length, all of which, put to their pur-pose, could spell out your alias ("Big Daddy," "Pink Lady," "Dr. Love") somewhere on your vehicle of choice.

My initial reaction was, "Whoa. Cool." Then I caught myself. Lost, for a moment, in this little gift of an ad, I regained consciousness and remembered this was a car ad in a consumer magazine. I was ashamed for having been taken in by this sneaky little "value-added" promotion, for having my innocence exposed by this designer's trap. It was a gotcha moment, and I was humiliated. So I fought back. *Fuck this ad. It's stupid.* And I closed the mag. Then reopened it. Then closed it again and jotted notes.

Maybe the ad guys anticipate this defensive reaction, having observed such hostility in polls or focus groups. They may then expect a cooling-off period. If the ad or gimmick is cool enough, a viewer may return to it, tired, submissive, like an abused spouse dropping the charges and coming home. I've seen many of the other inventive Mini Cooper campaigns. I got, in a *New Yorker*, one of those little miniguidebooks that first came out and, in *Wired* again, I think, those scored-paper mini-fold-out cars. This is playful stuff. But getting you to play—or to behave, as opposed to believe, in any *immediate* way at all—is not the point of these ads. You don't ever have to make the cars or peel off the stickers for the ad to make its point.

And the point is the idea *as IDEA* of the ad. And the idea is
not a substantive one, not a controversial truth, but rather
a shallow one about what else an ad can be, a lark, a goof,
a whimsical indulgence meant to make you feel good not
about the product but about advertising itself, as if I'm
supposed to say, "Thanks, Mini Cooper, for making ads fun
again. And useful, too!" In fact, if you actually do play with
this stuff (read the minibook, make the toy cars, place the
stickers somewhere), you pretty quickly feel like an idiot,
and more so like an idiot when, even after, you are surprised to find that, on some level, you still think the IDEA
is cool.

These gimmicks are no different from any other ad in
contriving to persuade you that you are only as cool as
what you buy, even if what you buy is to buy into the cool
ideas of an ad campaign.

ART IN ADS. When known artworks from Mona Lisa to a
Led Zeppelin song are appropriated in ads, I groan. I groan
a little groan for the artist who needed the cash (living
artist or license holder), and I groan a big groan for being
at the mercy of companies that assume I'm so stupid as to
fall for their clumsy baits and switches. I feel it's a shame.
I feel this. Right or wrong, naïve or idealistic, I groan. Why?
I'm not even all that sure. I complain that graphic designs
in ads are lowest-common-denominator fluff, and then
I complain when ads incorporate da Vinci and rock 'n' roll.
What do I want? I don't know. I think I howl from within
a well. Powerless. Impotent. Is it really ethical behavior or
good design or humble corporations that I want, or is it,
instead, that I crave power for myself? I exercise that
power when I make things on my own. My own writing, my

own designs, my own art. I am not dead yet! But maybe I
expect too much. Ads are omnipresent, corporations men-
ace globally, the world is a mall—were this not true, I could
probably let it all go, be quiet in my own place, be earnest
in my own ergonomic chair. But it is everywhere, and I
have to react somehow. I am forced to react. And I defend
myself. This is self-defense, in both senses of both words.
I am defending my very self. Step one. Step two, I must
assert myself. I react against them in order to act for myself. And then someone, somewhere, will react against me.

THE STATES OF OUR MINDS. What do designers believe about
what they have created, and what do designers believe
about the audience?
   It's possible that a designer can be one of three states of
mind, namely: (1) stupid, (2) cynical, or (3) hopeful.

1. Stupid
> (a) stupid enough to believe their own b.s.
> (b) stupid enough to believe the audience is stupid
> enough to believe their b.s.

2. Cynical
> (a) cynical enough to believe that the audience is
> used to b.s., and a b.s.-accustomed audience quick-
> ly becomes cynical about power as well as meaning,
> that is, a meaning-cynical audience devolves into
> a power-cynical audience, e.g. *a person who no
> longer thinks critically will no longer act critically*,
> thus abandoning all hope for the comfort of
> cynicism.
> (b) cynical enough to believe that the audience

knows all ads are b.s. but, rather than grumpily surrendering *a la* (2a) to this state of affairs, instead *welcomes & celebrates* all reduction of meaning into symbol, identity into brand, because it's head-in-the-sand easier and happy-go-lucky funner to just relax and rely on surface distinctions among the pretty colors and shapes (of logos, uniforms, slogans, the determined gait of Tiger Woods, the Boopsy charm of Jessica Simpson).

3. Hopeful

(a) hopeful enough to be blissfully optimistic, i.e. designers know the dynamic but underestimate the obstacles and happily never focus on results. (b) hopeful enough to be rationally pessimistic, i.e. designers know exactly what they're up against, but they keep trying anyway because no one ever said life wasn't shit and so what's to lose except losing?

It occurs to me to compile a *Kama Sutra*-type list in which all varieties of designers are paired with all varieties of audiences. Can a Designer (3b) communicate effectively to an Audience (2a)? Is the best partner for a Designer (1b) an Audience (2b)? Can a designer poll a sample of the target market to determine audience beliefs which would dictate what belief system a designer should adopt when crafting the design? And is such a designer who is capable of adopting at will multiple personae necessarily a Designer (2a or b), or could such a designer also be a Machiavellian Designer (3b)?

An empirical study more interesting to designers would

investigate whether being a designer of any type (any belief system, persona/ae) has any real effect on the style and/or content of the designs. Belief systems surely affect a designer's experience of work and of life (the inside perspective), but do belief systems necessarily affect the designs themselves (the outside expressions)? If one could correct for big factors like talent, experience, preferences, habits, etc., one might be able to craft a study in which the conclusion meant something. And if the conclusion were *no, designer beliefs make no difference*, I would expect Designers (1) to be confused then distracted, Designers (3) to be disappointed then determined, and Designers (2) to shrug and say, *We told you so.*

REGARDING THE ADOPTION OF NEW BELIEFS. It's tough to make a design meaningful. Images are shiny, language is empty. That makes it tough to escape cynicism and tougher to remain hopeful and committed. In this hard-to-breathe atmosphere, the designer then has to negotiate among the above three states of mind (well, two, since Designer (1) isn't really a choice, unless *willful ignorance* counts as Stupid, but being that it's willful makes the designer more of a Designer (2a)). And once a designer's self-conception loses its footing to the slipperiness of unmeaning, then designers can enrobe and disrobe themselves in beliefs according to the season's fashions. Designers can be as wily and promiscuous with their identities as their designs can be with symbols.

Consider the way in which companies respond to the latest trends in beliefs. *We don't expect you to believe we're a company that* actually *believes in equal-opportunity employment, environmentally sound practices, and fair*

labor, the company basically admits to the basically intelligent consumer slash stockholder. *Instead, we're a company
that expects you to believe that we're a company that* says
we believe in these things.

Because we are none of us idiots, we realize that companies drive very slowly, steering habitually toward the
well-worn short cuts of profitability, and always with reactionary swerves away from the slick new highways of
cultural so-called progress. But they are no dummies. They
know they have to respond in some way when consumer
complaint achieves a critical mass of demand. At some
point, it's just cheaper to go with the flow—or to say,
rather, that one is resolved to working toward implemen-
tation of a going-with-the-flow policy, the first proof
of commitment being this little logo here, this ribbon, this
letter from the president posted in the hallway near the
restrooms.

So, likewise, by verbally supporting one side of an issue
(pro-multiculturalism, pro-environment, etc.), many
designers behave, in a sense, like companies. Designers
don't expect you to believe they practice these beliefs, only
that they're the kind of designers who *say* they do. They
invest as little of themselves into rooting for child laborers
as they do rooting for a basketball team. If their team
makes it into the playoffs or their cause onto CNBC, hey,
that feels really good, and, well, that's the end of that. It's
belief as logo, politics as lapel pin. Self-promoters can sniff
a trend and surf public opinion without making the mistake of committing themselves one way or another. It's the
feeling, stupid. Not the act.

And the more abstract a position, the better, because it
allows a designer to be for the general notion at all times

*while preserving the flexibility to avoid every specific oppor-
tunity to act on it.*

And this is, too, exactly how companies think and oper-
ate, jabbing and feinting like a veteran pugilist.

*Yes, we're for It, we've always said we're for It, and we
deeply regret being unable to—hands tied here—do anything
further about It in this instance, or that one either, but
never having ever done anything about It doesn't in any way
change our global position on the Issue, which is to take It
into account always and always to first be saying we're
thinking about how best to secure the competitive future of
our Company and our People, that's our main responsibility
and we believe should be our main responsibility and so we
say that it is and hope you're hearing us saying that it is
because that's what's important, your hearing us strong
and clear on this Issue.*

This is more than concern about hypocrisy, hypocrisy
being as common in our commerce as hot air in a dirigible.
Hypocrisy is at times unavoidable, if not necessary for
growth, and besides, as Emerson said, a foolish consistency
is the hobgoblin of little minds.[†] What is more worrisome
is the circumstance in which all beliefs flit loose, no more
substantial than streamers behind a candidate, no more
signifying a probability of future action than wearing
a Yankees jersey means you'll be pitching tonight. Beliefs
falsely held make of you a hypocrite. The belief that
hypocrisy is inevitable makes of you a cynic. A society
of cynics makes of society a herd of grim cows, pathetic
in acquiescence.

---

† From the 1841 essay "Self-Reliance," by Ralph Waldo Emerson.

SKEPTICISM VS. CYNICISM. Don't confuse cynicism with skepticism. You might have just today learned how political consultants manipulate the media by tipping off journalists to stories damaging to opposing candidates. This could make you distrust everything politicians say, everything the media says, and everything—what the hell—anyone says about anything. That would be good. Distrust, that is. *Skepticism.* Cynicism, though, is not good. Cynicism takes a fresh skepticism and sours it into an across-the-board self-inflicted fuck-it-all. Cynics say things like *What did you expect* and *It doesn't make any difference.* Skeptics, on the other hand, possess active working minds anchored by the belief in objective standards. Skeptics care. Cynics don't. Cynics shut down their minds, deploy the same cavalier dismissal against any outcome, and believe in nothing but the worst in everyone; they only acknowledge, in the sick-and-tired voice of a race announcer who's seen it all, the subjective standard currently running well in the polls.

THE TROUBLE WITH TRYING ACTUALLY NOT TO TOTALLY BE CYNICAL. Designers are not unique in being tempted by the easy breezy ways of cynicism. We are all tempted. We are all at risk. And it's not just about being willing to believe anything in order to fit in at the conference, to be popular at work, to be liked by your clients. That bargain never satisfies. It's also about how difficult it is when one is actually not cynical but, instead, genuinely committed, however reasonably, to making good now and then on one's beliefs.

And we're not talking about a designer-saint or a pure simpleton, someone no more intellectually adept or morally sophisticated than young kids at that self-righteous age when they love to catch you breaking your own rules. The tough assignment is to compromise: to negotiate reasonably between your conscience and your bank account; to get what you want without getting fired; to do what you think is right without being so inflexible that no one wants to hire you. And even then, there are no guarantees. Even compromises you thought were reasonable turn out, in the end, to be nothing more than additional weights tipping the scale toward Cynicism.

Consider the following.

Question: Which designer gets the job?

(a) The good-faith designer who says he's for sustainable design, eco-friendly materials, fair labor practices, multiculturalism, union print shops, and then goes so far as to actually insist on paying the extra cost in effort, money and time all this commitment requires and, therefore, submits an honestly estimated bid.

(b) The crony designer who remains a crony in good standing because he says he's for all these goody-two-shoes things in general but will never sacrifice the bottom line (his, quietly, or his client's, loudly) for the "empty formalism" of ideological obedience, thus submitting lowball bids knowing Fate will be kind to him and adjust his profit margins in "unpredictable" and/or "unforeseeable" ways which turn out unforeseeably to increase the actual cost of the job beyond (a)'s quote, unpredictably.

Answer: Let us not praise naïve designers.

DECADENCE. The decadence of graphic design might be identified by the belief in the impotence of design and the inevitability of corporate power; by a disgust at our own reliance on consumerism for fulfilling psychological and spiritual yearnings; and by deferring to polls as the voice of the people and statistics as the language of Nature.

PARADOX. For the above reasons, independent work by graphic designers holds the most promise for satisfying a yearning for freedom of expression and holds the most possibility for unveiling this expression to the public in a forum outside of the funhouse, if only in a makeshift tent on the outskirts of the fairgrounds. Exercising a measure of control over the context in which you sell your work reinforces your commitment to controlling the meaning of your work, but it also requires salesmanship you may be unwilling or unprepared to perform. While you can, for once, bring to bear your personal design sensibility to the enterprise from product development to sales, you may be exhausted by the demands on your time, the new obstacles to success, and the lack of satisfaction you get from doing these other tasks ancillary to your main love.[21] You may come to appreciate those who do this work you once so disdained, and you may pine for the simple servitude of your old job, which now seems the pure and honorable calling you once dreamed of answering. But you should, no matter what, gain what can be gained when one dares to try something new; that is, you will reap the benefits that accrue to the self-taught.

The paradox is that, if one embraces this outsider strategy, then, at the very moment of satisfaction, *one ceases to be a graphic designer at all*. The secret off-hours work, in other words, is well and good for those okay with finding satisfaction outside of their jobs and simpatico with working in the limbo of non-designation or hybrid designation (artist/designer/creator/entrepreneur). But in considering how to implement all this within the designer's daily glut of assigned projects, within the world in which the client relationship is a defining element, then we are coming round and round again to the question, *What is a graphic designer, as a graphic designer, to do?!*

[A] **MORE IS THE SAME.** A designer might get involved earlier in the process the way plant workers are sometimes asked for input on the purchase and installation of new equipment for the line. The justification for this is that the anticipated gains in quality, safety, and efficiency will, in the language of the manufacturing sector today, boost the competitiveness of the company and thus increase job security for the workers. This is no answer, however, to the main concern of the worker or designer, and in fact suggests its opposite: that the solution for graphic designers is to expand their duties in order to become *less like graphic designers.*

Expanding the definition of graphic designer surely requires a revaluing of the job description, which might require an expansion of duties as well as a rejection of certain obligations, but little progress is made if the consequence of the expansion is merely to slide the designer up and down the vertical trunk of the job tree, toward the branches of market research or the roots of product development. The dynamics remain the same: dancing to the client's tune in the fairy-tale ballroom of the marketplace. Auto workers, for example, care about manufacturing process but aren't encouraged to confront engineers or the marketing department to propose changes to the product, the materials it's made of, or the way it's sold. For designers to influence decisions at analogous levels, they might, as has been suggested,[22] install themselves in board rooms and on committees, in business-development forums and in community groups. This hearkens back to the point about careerism, opportunism, and the imperative to get up, smile, and kiss ass: an ambitious notion with the virtue of optimism but, at this level, an avenue open to very few. Pursue this, heartily, do. The rest of us, however, need urgently to establish who we are, why we care, and what work we are capable of.

Industry and professional leadership, furthermore, depends upon good minds inhabiting the suits these roles provide. To represent, one must know what one is representing. One must have *already redefined* the role of the graphic designer—if not also reached consensus in the field about this redefinition—in order to promote the new ideal!

[B] GET A JOB. Complaints about the clients one works for and the products and services for which one is designing may be addressed, if one is so disposed, with brutal frankness: quit bitching and get a job. Design for a political journal or a magazine with whose manifesto you sympathize. Do editorial illustrations and cartoons. Interview with firms and institutions whose mission statements inspire in you twitches of solidarity. Consider moving to another state, if necessary. Start your own studio with a crew of like-minded souls. While the heart beats and the lungs inflate, your body is still made for working. Do so. And keep in mind that the formula of new job + new boss + new client won't necessarily = a happier, stronger you. The conflicts of the graphic designer will dog you, like obsession, wherever you go. This caution is not meant to counsel defeatism but to remind you to keep your antennae tuned to the right frequencies. The big questions have hard answers, lifelong in the pursuit.

[C] GETTING AWAY WITH IT. When considering a project, I wonder how far I can follow my inclinations before the client says, "I don't get it," in which simple case I need only offer a plausible exegesis without insulting the client's discernment. If, however, the client says, "Hey, what do you think you're doing," the client likely suspects I have hijacked his project for my own ends, and I must either play dumb or capitulate, knowing in either case that it was worth the try—and that I'll surely try again on the next project.

OBJECTION. *I work in a fast-paced prepress shop, and I barely have time for the snack truck, let alone the luxury to indulge in pursuits of the kind you're advocating.*

REPLY. I hear you. I work for a union print shop in Detroit, and all year long the graphic designers there design and typeset newsletters, calendars, magazines, yearbooks, training manuals, direct-mail flyers, and business cards for union locals, the Big Three, and liberal political organizations whose constituents insist on the union bug. I think, like you do, that most designers (if not most workers in general) are overworked, underpaid, saddled with grunt-work, and rarely challenged creatively *(can't you just make this look like* Time *or* Newsweek?). So I expect that, yes, they'd think I was doing nothing more than irritating them with a poor Woody Allen impersonation, whining and moaning, a doctor with a diagnosis but no prescription, and if I really wanted to be helpful, I would take a seat and prep this file for the Indigo.

Of course, you need only surf the web to verify that some designers are already hairy-armed and fang-toothed, howling like the monsters I am describing, making their beastly progress across the moonlit prairies of trial and error. They're out there. Believe it.

Within one's daily practice, by contrast, it is possible that the opportunity for self-determination arises in no more than one out of twenty projects at best. But like the weekend, chocolate, and sex, it makes it possible to go on.

BOTTOM LINE. It might come down to how you choose to define The Good Life; whether you choose—to the best of your ability, talent and opportunity—to live it; and how much you are willing to sacrifice—in money, time and prestige—to keep it.

OH, AND ANOTHER THING; CONSIDER IT [D] ROLE GENERATION. There is one other possibility that I'm probably a little late off the starting blocks in considering. There might be a simple solution to this problem of cramming a new soul into the old body of graphic design without exploding that body into unrecognizable pulp. And that is more bodies.

Dr. Frankenstein made a monster way before there was genetic engineering, cloning, or the celebration of free-market incentives. We got it easy. Just come up with some new role, one that combines graphic design with other disciplines (oh, I don't know, law and writing come to mind, and also anthropology, medicine, engineering), and maybe eventually we'll grow accustomed to these new roles and regard them not as hybrids but as things in themselves.

Maybe it won't be so weird to have writer/designers write and design books for clients, anthropologist/designers create and design their own multicultural-training programs for corporations, or statistician/designers crunch the numbers and design their own graphs. This happens to some extent today. Designers enter other professions. Other professionals get into design. Designers, writers, lawyers, academics and everyone else focus in on narrow fields of expertise often defined by a hybridization.

But the hybrid designer is likely the rare anomaly in a marketplace otherwise defined by specialization and division of labor. Clients are used to dealing with teams, firms, and departments and (in my limited experience) are distrustful of jacks-of-all-trades and renaissance superheroes. I often don't tell the client that I'm the one doing all the writing, photography and design for a given project because it suggests (a) that I won't do as good a job; (b) that if I do a good job, it'll make them look lazy in their own jobs; and (c) that maybe if it's just one guy instead of three, they can pay me two-thirds less.

The market being the market, however, means it must accept a good idea like a kid swallowing a spinach pill. And if you can play the game by crafting a niche for yourself as a hybrid designer with a cool new name and by backing up your brand with unique expertise clients will pay for, well, hell, I guess that kind of packs the bag and boots this problem out the door. At least for those particular probably-still-rare folks. But new hybrid roles, once defined and in existence, can attract new takers among students, the curious, and those who've been waiting years for something like this to come along.

WHAT IT MEANS TO BE A GREAT DESIGNER. As an example
of how designers struggle with identifying themselves and
their work (a struggle to which I am no stranger, obviously), I cite Paul Rand's foreword for the book, *Zero: Hans
Schleger—A Life of Design*.

"Schleger was not a typical commercial artist," writes
Rand. "This is not to say that he lived in an ivory tower, nor
that his work was merely *artistic*."

The italics are Rand's. I have read these lines many
times, and I'm still not sure what to make of them. Rand
wants to place Schleger in a category of his own, ahead of
his time, "a graphic designer before the concept of graphic
design was invented" (not sure what the significance of
this is either since Zero (1898-1976) was not the first guy
to have devoted his life to commercial art), "one of the
first to pioneer modern design as we know it today," an
intellectual who was not an *ivory-tower* academic (he
never taught in a college but, rather, taught art-school
grads informally in his home studio, which he apparently
enjoyed), an artist who did not make *art*, a commercial
artist who was not *typically commercial*.

"Keenly concerned with questions of aesthetics, he was
equally concerned with problems of business," Rand continues. "He was as versed in the art of selling as he was in
the art of Art."

It seems to me designers almost without fail endure
a peculiar strain when writing about design, a kind of professional identity crisis, an insecurity *(I'm not just a
designer)* counterbalanced by a vanity *(I'm more than an
artist)*. Designers, apparently, have never been happy with
their *name*. Designers deploy their art on behalf of commerce. The duality *is* the definition. It might very well be

that designers themselves are at fault for making such a big deal out of their own insecurities. "You are what you are," one might say. "Deal with it."

I believe, however, that designers' ambivalence about their own roles and self-definitions should be maintained, encouraged, the hands wrung as long as there are hands to wring. This ambivalence is something most people feel —whether as writers, lawyers, doctors, or whatever. Why? Because we are more than our jobs. Who among us has not felt constrained and powerless in our jobs? The power-lessness provokes us to ask questions. *For whom am I working? Why am I working? If I am what I do, who am I?* If only everyone were as insecure as designers and asked themselves these questions over and over, they would be forced to cobble together some answers, to make a few surprising choices, judgments they would never have made had they taken their *given* names for granted.

Questioning your role is also one way to contest your relationships. It is one way to express skepticism about the motives and goals of the company you're working for. It is one way to take stock of the consequences of your actions. It is one way to lift your head from the sand . . . .

There are deeper issues than whether or not, to praise designers, one must call them *artists,* or whether or not, to insult artists, one need only call them *designers* (and *vice versa*). One such issue is what it means to be a great designer, period . . . .

It would be an achievement to praise someone as a great designer without having to sneer at artists or academics to do so. One tribe sneers at another. The tribal instinct breeds resentment, which, in the case of designers, is fueled by confusion over the very boundaries of the tribe,

over what criteria an outsider must meet to be invited
to the insiders' campfire. Resentment is also bred by self-
pity. I pity my lot in life and, in revenge, resent, loudly, the
greener grass of the lots next door. The contributions of
graphic designers are undervalued because most people
have no idea what designers do. Thus, designers pine to
be more well-known.

In an essay on Speak Up,[23] the design blog he hosts,
Armin Vit writes, "If you ask me, there are far too many
people without the proper qualifications claiming to be
graphic designers . . . . Ideally a graphic designer is trained,
educated and introduced to the profession through a design
program . . . . The grand question then: Must a designer be
subjected to a list of bullet points to be considered one?
Therein lies the problem as well as the beauty of diversity
many (as well as I) argue for because the answer is no."

Thankfully Vit backs away from insisting on I.D. check-
points at the borders of Design. We're not talking about
practicing medicine here. We should rely on the market—
shouldn't we?—to distinguish great from mediocre talents,
on the theory that all that education—all that accumula-
tion of qualifications—should be worth something in the
commercial world.

After fretting over the proper credentialing of graphic
designers, one may fret over the proper disposition of
graphic designers, that is, over what face designers show
to the world. Should design be a business or a profession?
Clement Mok, in a column for the May/June 2004 issue of
Communication Arts, posits that "designers are currently
a divided, fractious lot, whose professional esteem is con-
siderably lower than it should be" and that, as either a
cause or effect of designers failing to make the design pro-

fession better known and understood by clients, designers are "frequently excluded from participation in business enterprises except in a narrowly circumscribed, post-hoc context." He argues that designers should therefore "professionalize the profession" with, among other tactics, composing a "shared professional vocabulary and ethos."

His idealism is misplaced at a time when most professions—accounting, law and medicine, for example—have been deconstructed into businesses. The professional model has long since given way to the reign of the business model. It would be a quixotic endeavor to reverse this trend and remake design, which has always been based on a business model, into a profession. People tend to loathe professions anyway, for precisely what Mok values in them. A "shared professional vocabulary" has in practice resulted in elitist jargon meant to keep outsiders at bay, confused and dependent on the initiated to interpret for them. Popular resentment of the legal profession (now a business) still generates countless lawyer jokes.

To cover all designers under the umbrella of a single explanation of what designers do, as Mok advocates, would require such an abstract generalized claim that it would likely be as meaningless as "I help people" is to doctors or "I practice law" is to lawyers (or "I write" is to writers). Doctors, lawyers and accountants specialize in certain areas because the depth of expertise requires it and because it is financially rewarding to do so. This enables them to explain what it is they do in clear concise statements. Designers, however, commonly need to offer a broader range of services—both horizontally (among media) and vertically (within the project)—in order to survive.

Designers come in all stripes, all levels of talent, with vocabularies and creeds of all sorts, and they react to the evolving needs of the commercial world in order to continue serving their clients. Designers endure because they adapt to what their clients demand, flourish because they imagine what their clients cannot. Let a committee adopt a slogan, standardize an ethos in the minutes, and the echo of the achievement will die before it reaches the hallway.

I should emphasize that I'm not dissing any particular methodology or strategy in particular. Mok cites with approval the three-phase design process delineated by the American Institute of Graphic Arts (AIGA), a process drawn from case study, but while Mok wants to rely on the process as prescriptive (what all designers should do and adopt), I regard it as merely descriptive (what some designers have done and what others might do, if they wanted). That's the difference. Designers should assert themselves against any imposed orthodoxy. It's what all the great artists, writers and designers do. It's in the blood.

And therein lies one argument for the instrumental value of insisting on the adoption of an industry-wide creed: *that designers will rebel against it*, and some good will come of that rebellion.

Whatever path you take to get to the practice of design, you will likely confront the current generation's venerated and mighty oak tree whose gnarled leafy branches spell out **WHAT IT MEANS TO BE A GREAT DESIGNER**. And the irony is that to be a great designer you might have to destroy what it has meant for others to be a designer, and to redefine what it can now mean for you to be a designer.

GREATEST HITS OF THE AESTHETIC VENDETTAS, VOL. I. So far, I have been babbling on about (a) the circumstances in which the designer designs, such as the job in particular and the market in general, (b) the psychology of the designer designing within these circumstances, (c) the ethical and moral dimensions of this work, and (d) the exploration of new ways of thinking and working as a designer, folding into this batter the butter and sugar of other disciplines like law and writing. While I have likely not sidestepped self-indulgence, I have so far avoided nose-diving into the quicksand of aesthetics. Whenever I have been tempted to leave the straight and narrow, I have heard, in the trees, the cautionary *a cappellas* of that infamous bird choir, the Aesthetic Vendettas, in particular their second and third hits, "Ooh, You Better Check Yourself" and "Boy, You Don't Know Shit."

But I have diagnosed in myself as a designer moodiness and ill temper and have roughly identified the causes as (a) a queasiness with the decorative, (b) a denial of disposability, and (c) a faith in The Cool. These are, obviously, interrelated, since the decorative is disposable, and appeals to The Cool seek to elide the finer aesthetic distinctions, short-circuit further thought, and deny the disposability of one's work. Putting faith in The Cool (as in, "Man, I don't know why I like it, it just looks cool") often accelerates productivity in an attempt to keep self-criticism at bay. To be prolific is to be saved by numbers, which should remind you of that old salesman's joke about what we lose on individual sales we make up in volume. Fear of accusations that one's work is merely decorative and therefore disposable is what drives the designer into having faith in The Cool.[24] But neither the religion of The Cool nor any other aesthetic religion can rescue us from the facts of life. Our work as individuals is limited by our fate as a species. You and I will not overcome death, genetic engineering notwithstanding, and every species, dependent as it is on planetary habitability, will one day succumb to the expiration of its Use-By Date.

Acknowledgment of our mortality should not, however, require us to retreat into total nihilism and the reckless abandonment of all value judgments (or the desperate production of gigantic monographs and survey tomes which by bulk alone hope to dissuade Death from stopping by). It is merely an acknowledgment of the circumstances in which all of us live and work. Mortality is, in a sense, our container, but we have not emptied our container by virtue of having described its shape. Our very lives have aesthetic dimension—time, space, matter and energy being the forms in which we are appreciated and, by way of our self-consciousness, appreciate ourselves. Such is our vessel.

Aesthetic religions misinterpret our human condition and therefore our artistic condition and, in fear, entreat us from stepping off into the godless oblivion of anything goes by soothing us with balms of call and response, prayer and assurance, obedience and reward. If we follow, we shall be saved. It is a promise that cannot be kept based on a belief that cannot be sustained. No one's work is salvaged from the ruin of Time by mere adherence to Modernism or devotion to Paul Rand. (As students should be graded on their answers to the exam, not on how well they looked turning it in, so designers should be judged according to the form and content of their work, not on how faithfully they recited a catechism.) Aesthetic religions have not been an adequate answer to how to create, just as religions have not been an adequate answer to how to live. Consider the exhortations to make it messy,[25] keep it clean, use photographs, rely on illustration, defer to tradition, make it new, always follow this rule,[26] never listen to that guy (he's a crackpot), you can't go wrong doing what she says (she's a genius). General prescriptions offend the individual taste and always disappoint the particular circumstance. Thus:

BEWARE OF DOGMA.

Injunctions from a self-appointed authority to emulate the seven effective habits of successful designers are laughable for being awkward, self-serving, and inflexible; they are either so generally stated as to be useless or so absurdly specific as to be useful only as provocation, bait for the bored. The aesthetic religion is doomed to stasis, vulnerable to breach, and fated for obsolescence, any particular one surviving as a historical curiosity, a closet to sort through when one wishes to play dress up. The surest way to incite resistance is to codify an aesthetic style. Build a statue of your saint, and pigeons will find expression for their dissent.

GREATEST HITS OF THE AESTHETIC VENDETTAS, VOL. II.
It might be that small embattled groups found aesthetic religions for fear of absorption into the majority's religion, or that majorities found them in contempt for the insouciance of a minority. Either way or both, their establishment tends to exacerbate, if not demarcate the battleground for, unproductive cultural warfare. So I focus on the individual. Christ, to paraphrase Nietzsche, was the only

true Christian.[†] You must work to become yourself.
You can't buy a personality by submitting to off-the-rack
ideology.

So where might this work start? Appreciate, for a
moment, what resources await the individual, to whom,
today, so much of history is accessible by hyperlink, data-
base, online bookstore, or local library. History empowers
designers no less than writers, academics, philosophers,
or, for that matter, all enthusiastic citizens. Designers will,
say, delve into the history of the opera for which they are
designing a poster, the company for which they are designing a brochure, or a museum for which they are designing
a catalog. But, for reasons of expedience, they are unlikely
to expand their investigation beyond the particular history, whereas I am interested in what all history promises
for the designer, from the history of cocaine to the history
of conquest. Designers should make use of this history,
and not just art history but anthropology, archaeology, the
Sumerians, the history of North American mammals, the
dinosaurs, Machiavelli, inventions, disease, Shakespeare
and the steam engine, the Cheyenne and the bison, small-
pox, rice farming, continental drift, the history of the
Roman Empire, and the child warriors of Africa.

Two seconds ago is as much the past as two centuries
ago, but few need to be reminded to give credence to living
memory. The unknown or disregarded histories deserve
attention, the 1920s as well as the 1290s. Unconsidered,
unimagined perspectives increase your sensitivity to what
has changed in the world and what has remained constant

---

† "There was only one Christian and he died on the cross." See
Aphorism 39, *The Antichrist* (1895), Friedrich Nietzsche.

in human nature. Cultures, politics, arts and sciences await retrieval, interpretation, and the transportation into relevance.

History contains the seeds of inspiration for designers today. Treasures lie dormant in the crypt. This is where aesthetics has something to do with all that history, narrative, language, and truth I was on about before.

Embrace heresy.

Raid the tombs.

GREATEST HITS OF THE AESTHETIC VENDETTAS, VOL. III. What criteria obtain when scavenging for meaningful aesthetics in the heap of history? A certain randomness might be necessary at first, a certain recklessness and exuberance and the license, now and then, of saying to oneself, *"Why not?"* It's a process of approach and acceptance, a process of seduction, a curiosity born of loneliness. One, eventually, discovers an interest in a particular history or in particular facts throughout history—flashes and glints in the heap—the hit-and-miss way one slowly determines the kind of work one wants to do. You keep trying until something strikes you, plucks a chord in the lute of your heart (or mixes the right beat into the track of your brain). Thereafter, you examine the gem through the filters of your values, values that help you reject and select what about these histories you can apply in your own designs. You can't control what inspires you, but you can choose what to feed your inspiration as well as what inspiration you choose to act on. I may not be able to explain why a certain design solution occurred to me, for example, but I should be able to account for my investigations (into the history of crustaceans and medieval armature, etc.). And, more importantly, I should be able to explain my reasons for *using this solution above all others.*[27]

ANOTHER DIGRESSION, BACKSLIDING INTO AESTHETICS.
It's possible I should've applied this rule (see last sentence) more strictly to this reckless sprawl of an essay. Maybe it suffers from insufficient editing, but, then again, maybe I should've burned the whole thing down. Which reminds me: you can tell when someone doubts their piece of writing because they'll resort to claiming it as a catalyst to further dialogue, as if they'd walked nude into a costume party, instantly regretted having been brave enough to dare, and then excused themselves to depart, head high, out the door, embracing the consolation that the subject of their nudity will absolutely dominate the party's conversation for the next three hours. The self-doubting writer's hope, in other words, is that the essay might compensate for a lack of intrinsic value by offering instrumental value, that is, getting a reaction, which usually means getting people so worked up they have to write back in complaint. A poking stick don't need to be pretty to get folks to jump.

It is this instrumental effect for which designers, I suspect, are valued: to spur action, to affect behavior. And it is also why graphic design itself can take so many forms and, thus, resist the confines of aesthetic pronouncements. Aesthetics have to do with intrinsic value, with the way things relate to each other on the page, screen, other surface or space; the aesthetic value of a design does not depend on how or whether it affects the way viewers relate to each other in the world. That value is instrumental. You can design a gorgeous package whose function is unclear and whose operation is defeated by its very design—and people will appreciate it but will be unable to use it. You can also design a butt-ugly gadget whose function is conveniently obvious and whose operation is plain to a monkey—and people will appreciate it but *not want* to use it. These are different values, each prized more or less depending on the marching orders.

A design that combines these two values in harmonious relation (whether one value is greater than the other or they are in balance) is the mark of success. Wait. I take that back. I employed that lazy adjective *harmonious* without defining it, and now that I've noticed I've committed this common crime, I must backpedal and plead insanity: to define *harmony* in order to play it as an aesthetic trump card is to ask of the term too much. A design can be off-kilter, asymmetrical, or imbalanced; it's not structural or physical proportion that is the concern. The goal is to reckon a relationship (harmonious or otherwise) between the aesthetics of the design and the instrumental power of the design, and while one design may give the edge to aesthetics, the next may sacrifice aesthetics for instrumental purpose.

EFFICIENCY WITHIN THE DESIGN. To rely on *harmony* as some kind of magic gauge of aesthetic value is a cop-out, and to do so—to be caught in that cop-out—is to sprint to the tautological home bases of *balance* and *efficiency*. Ah, efficiency. Sounds so much harder and tougher than *harmony*. More manly. More scientific. Reliably measurable. Verifiably supportable.

Efficiency: optimal resource-allocation; *optimal* to be understood as an unattainable ideal and not as a description of the real world; a value not tied to any system but which can be applied to any system.

Consider efficiency as a value in the critique of a design. Critics often explicitly admire a design's "efficient use of space/color/line" or else imply efficiency as the standard by citing infractions of messiness, sloppiness, a waste of resources, a squandering—which is pretty much the impulse of humanity. One could argue our consumer culture is driven by the desire to acquire and the need to expire, and to admire *efficiency* is to implicitly perpetuate this cycle (by perfecting an input/output *harmony* of energy). Our guilt about our mucking up of where we live might be what drives us to conceal the evidence, to prevent our sinful natures from finding expression in our artwork and to disparage such expression when made manifest. We disgust ourselves every day; must we remind ourselves of this disgust in our art? Such is the guilt. And such is waste and decay the subversion of it, the messiness, which becomes, by insisting on the mess we have made, a sociopolitical statement, one that maybe says, to ourselves, *This is who we are*, and, to authority, *You will not get away with this.*

Consumption is a vicious cycle that the eco-sustainability movement—itself guilt-ridden by what humans can muck up but optimistically pragmatic about what responsibility and accountability can accomplish—can only slow or temper but not stop or counteract. Human beings are what is between a mouth and an asshole, our elegant amalgams of flesh and imagination bent to the purpose of turning flora and fauna into frenzy and feces. Our minds dream of heaven, while our bodies are delivery systems for shit. On a larger scale is society, a macrocosm of the human devourer and defecator. Faith in efficiency, like faith in religion, is faith in the absolutions of superior hygiene. Make us better than ourselves. Undirty our minds, our feet, bleach our dreams and our underwear. Pure of body, heart and soul, speckless and unstained, as sterile as the pin on which the unnumbered angels alight. Cleanliness is next to, etc.

It is this cleanliness—the technocratic efficiency, the hygienic spirit—that informs our judgments about what makes design elegant, high-class, sophisticated, confident, superior, disdainful of what it is not: loud, coarse, dirty, bodily, and desperate for attention. Clean type, soothing colors, flawless skin. It is what we are not that we revere as the ideal. And it is this ideal that is defined as that which is not us. To step toward an Ideal, one must step away from one's self; to do that, one must be self-conscious and self-critical and—the crucial step—self-*disgusted*. It is an impossible ideal, suprahuman, self-hating, and contemp-tuous of the lower classes, those who cannot afford the luxury of superior mental hygiene. It is the aesthetic equivalent of suicide. This kind of art kills us to show us what we can be in death. We burn our bodies, mourn false selves, and celebrate unbeing. The deader, the better. Let us be clouds.

But to opt reflexively for the aesthetic equivalent of the Rabelaisian delight in the grotesqueries of the human body is to cede artistic self-control to reactionary recklessness, to the rebel's abandon, as if in reaction against popular illusion one always finds expression for one's individual reality. This is false. Objecting to sun-worshippers, you don't then worship the mud. Instead, you don't *worship* at all. For art and design to retain meaning, the artist/design-er must retain control. Choice must be informed and conscious, even the choice to depict chaos.

And a reflexive solipsism must be avoided. The world

is more than the self. There is an objective external reality beyond our subjective internal experience. To judge all aesthetics according to a solipsistic POV is to anthropo-morphize the thing you're looking at, making the clean pale rigid forms on a page into the printed equivalent of our spiritual aspirations. This might be the artist's/design-er's intent, admittedly. But it might not. And, still, you can take this clean/dirty, superior/inferior, god/human dialec-tical aesthetics and apply it to the thing-world as well. A house can be new and white and as picture-perfect as a 1950's auto advertisement. Or it can be run-down with a backed-up toilet, a leaky roof, a third mortgage, and a divorce-in-progress in the back bedroom. Ideal vs. real? Glass half empty vs. half full? Even the run-down "more realistic" household can be demoted to the running joke in a family sitcom or Farelly Brothers flick. And third, fourth and fifth cases can be combinations of the two artificially concocted types, types whose categorical borders shatter like sugar glass when reality is subjected to long hard bouts of investigation & discernment.

Being aware of the ghosts in the forest enables the artist/designer to navigate a path, choosing routes of varying degrees of dappled shade and murky bend. Again, we return to the artist's/designer's meaningful informed choice & intent for guidance as to how one creates, while still recognizing the kinds of scrutiny that will be aimed at the work in its public context, when the work emerges from the forest into the searchlight's sweeping cone, the interrogator's bare-bulb glare, or the new season's soft refractive glow.

EFFICIENCY OUTSIDE THE DESIGN. Efficiency as an aesthetic value embodied within the design is something you as a designer might be interested in, but efficiency as an instrumental value is what mostly interests your clients. They want your design to *do* something: move product, raise awareness, save lives.

The client's dream of high efficiency—optimal resource-allocation—is basically that they get the most bang of consumer response for the least buck they can toss to you. Clients may, presumably, work backward from their desired consumer response « through the types of media best suited for the communication « to the designers/firms best positioned to achieve that consumer response via particular media. Indices for designer/firm comparisons probably vary with client and industry, and clients surely have all sorts of reasons for ultimately going with certain designers/firms over others.[28] That's less interesting than the issue of whether, if the commercially instrumental value of a design could be measured, clients would want to rely on that as the main index of comparison (for one thing, consider that when choosing a designer with a *lower* Adjusted Profitability Index Score, the client, consequently, would have some 'splaining to do to justify ignoring that low Index Score and going with a second-stringer). I don't want to take the analogy too far, but it's kind of like college admissions, with a designer's instrumental-value indices being equivalent to the high-school senior's hard numbers of grades and tests. Soft stuff still counts but as secondary considerations (and of course cronyism and nepotism are always in play[29]).

Designers tend not to evaluate peer work according to instrumental market criteria possibly for fear of indicting

themselves, calling attention to the designer's paradox:
context takes all, and this context was made for lying.
If you ignore context, authority, intent, and audience, and
just focus on aesthetics—the relationships within the
given frame—then you sidestep the paradox by ignoring it.
This opens up a way to appreciate the design outside of its
function, outside of its instrumental value. That instrumental value, presumably, is exactly why the design was
created in the first place—the designer hired by a client
for a specific job. Judging design by its instrumental value
would be to judge it by market-based indexes: customer
satisfaction, sales, profits, good-will generated, brand
recognition, etc. Which, I should clarify, is not the same as
incorporating awareness of context into aesthetic appreciation or into a synergistic appreciation of both aesthetic
and instrumental values; market-based indexes measure
consumption not interpretation.

Is someone working on building the equivalent of a J.D.
Powers survey with attendant awards for design? I haven't
heard of it, though I may be ignorant. With designers so
tired of hearing about commercial criticism and begging
critics to get over it and embrace the inevitable, you'd
think they'd do the same, put their money where their
designs are and subject their proudly instrumentally commercial designs to strictly instrumentally commercial
standards—meaning that the only good design is a successful design, no matter what it looks like, how it's disseminated, or what collateral damage it inflicts.

And if these market realists object, one has to wonder
why. *Commercial indexes don't exclude aesthetic ones,* they
might argue, *but rather support them by perhaps correlat-
ing aesthetic value with instrumental value and therefore*

validating our faith in aesthetics. This is romantic malarkey. Two reasons.

First, the commercial index will free clients (those who resent their dependence on creative types) from having to listen to designers blab on about intrinsic value. No business person will ever again have to feel dumb hearing big words he doesn't understand. It's just *show me the money*, i.e. poll it, focus-group it, market-test it, and if the job doesn't warrant the resources, then copy someone else's proven thing. Business sense is often risk-averse, and one way to reduce the risk of loss and increase the probability of gain is to go with proven things while waiting for the other guy to take a chance on the next hot thing which, once market-proven, provides just the kind of reassuring lullaby the decision-makers want to hear before they invest the resources and go ahead and copy someone else's proven thing.[30]

Second, the competition for higher numbers in the instrumental column becomes a race for attention, aesthetics be damned. Appreciating the aesthetics of a sophisticated, powerful, artistic design takes time and mental interpretive energy, two things highway drivers, TV watchers, and sidewalk shoppers don't pretend to have in anything like abundance. Be funny. Be cute. Be simple. Be digestible. Just don't be naïve about the dynamics of consumerism. And don't put on airs.

Aesthetic standards will always appeal to the design profession itself, however, and what ensues in that world is the emergence of predictable aesthetic/instrumental factions likely to paint their clubhouse doors with, say, *Aesthetics Forever!* or *Profit Now!* or *Reasonable Synergists for Inclusion & Liberty!* Great designs are like great artworks: ambiguous, ambivalent, self-critical, subject to deep and divided interpretations. Great designs, therefore, aren't likely to make great money (at least not right away). Aesthetic appreciation endures despite the verdicts of ephemeral commerce. No great designer will lack for the inspiring anecdote of the poor genius. But a great designer lives not on dream alone. Thus, a designer will be forced, more than ever, to respond to the client's insistence on market-defined instrumentalism (whatever sells) to the exclusion of good design (however defined).

The goal of optimal efficiency in the context of commercial design is, morally speaking, an empty one of ends, not means. The instrumental value—making something happen—trumps not only any aesthetic value (as just described) but, further, any moral restraint. In economics, they call it the problem of "moral monstrosity." It refers to the moral vacuity of efficiency calculations, whereby hospitals choose not to treat poor patients because their lives are not worth the investment, governments choose to kill suspected dissidents because it's cheaper than the costs of running a judicial system, and companies abduct their own citizens and enslave them in factories because cheap labor enables them to win First World contracts. Academics have discussed the necessity of making hard choices based on imperfect information: how do you know any given poor person won't discover a cure for cancer; a dissident lead the country to prosperity; an employee invent the product that saves the company? You don't. But the larger point is that what constitutes the relevant information, known or unknown, is the kind of information that would increase the precision in assessing *the instrumental value* of a person, an efficiency calculation of that person's contribution to society. The appreciation of a personality, of the individual as an individual, is not admitted as relevant. It'd be like a father shooting his son who lost an arm to the combine because a one-armed son, loved or unloved, isn't worth the room and board anymore. What makes life worth living? Do you have to charge a ticket price and put on a one-person show for someone to appreciate you as you?

Because we experience life as individuals, we are instinctively repelled by the valuations of our lives that must be made when making decisions on the basis of the most efficient society. We feel undervalued, disposable, and we resist it, deny our very mortality, because no amount of money is likely enough to make us sacrifice our life[31] (for reasonable people, anyway). But to acknowledge our mortality is not to trade it, to auction off our organs on eBay while we live. Inefficiency has its benefits. Life is itself inefficient.

And the irony of this economically idealistic way of weighing the world is that in practice we defer (we in developed countries) to the market to assign value because we don't trust our subjective selves, we who are handicapped by imperfect info and limited perspective. So now it is this imperfect engine of the market we trust, but only insofar as it can be controlled. We regulate it and monitor it, managing the moral monstrosities of illegal markets for slaves, drugs, girls, and kidneys, and keeping a lid on monopolies, price fixing, and insider trading.[32] Those empowered by cheating the market are the first to praise the market, that praise being a curtain of rhetorical smoke behind which power seeks to sustain itself indefinitely. Unchecked self-interest is no longer the *enemy* of social efficiency; it is now (supposedly) the *engine* of social efficiency. And it is dizzying to consider that when we started talking about efficiency we were worried about subordinating individual life to society's interests, and now, spinning out the practical consequences, we are here subordinating all of society's interests to the fiat of the few.

So how does efficiency's moral-monstrosity problem apply to design? Take the skeleton of the above para and drape it with the skin of the design world. We defer to the market to assign value to the design because we don't trust our subjective selves, either designers or clients, because we are handicapped by imperfect information and limited perspective (these two limitations reducing the efficacy and import of those instrumental-value indexes; in other words, we can't know everything because we can't see everywhere and so we can't calculate costs/benefits with objective accuracy and so we estimate as precisely as we can). And now it is this design market that we must control somehow, managing its tendencies to lead to moral monstrosities like:

1. **Fungible Designs:**[33] When the dollar is the only standard of value, everything is fungible, and fungible designs lead to strange inversions. Clients bargain not for the design itself but for its effects, and if your design falls short in causing the bargained-for effects, you only get paid the proportional amount. Leaving aside measurability issues, imagine your AIDS-awareness poster fails to raise awareness by some number; your magazine print ad fails to increase monthly sales; your *Hamlet* flyers succeed in filling only half the auditorium. Money is money, design is money, money is design, and so your

design is only as valuable as the money it makes.
Now take it farther: you bid for the project to raise
AIDS awareness, and your poster's failure to increase awareness may have cost lives that another
bidder's poster might have saved. If lives can be
valued in money, then money can be valued in
lives, and so your failure to save, say, six lives rep-
resents, say, $6 million for which you are
responsible. This is absurd, right? Even if you could
insure your designs against failures like this, it just
doesn't make sense. Does it? Make it about profits
instead of lives. Your failure to increase profits
cost the company. Maybe you're not responsible
for these profits, but maybe you are still responsible for what the company spent for your work.[34]
No effect. No pay. The only thing that differenti-
ates you from any other bidding designer is what
your design can do. All designs are fungible. And
so, to the client, are you.[†]

2. **glAMORALization**: In a free unregulated market in
which the only value is the instrumentally economic (money), design could promote and glamorize
pedophilia, rape, needle sharing, unprotected sex,
underage drinking, drinking and driving, xenophil-
ia, necrophilia, misogyny, cannibalism, terrorism,

---

† And what if you make *more* than the bargained-for amount? Do you
think the client would pay it? If you can contract for it in the way
of royalties or performance-based reward, then get it. Do. But more
likely you'll just win a little in the way of good will to be leveraged
upon the submission of the next bid.

car-bombing, plane-hijacking, the latest hate
crime, etc., and all with intent to sell related or
unrelated products or services (from drugs and
guns to slaves and child prostitutes).[†] It would be
anything-goes in design, whether the product/
service was illegal/immoral or, in more likely scenarios, the illegal/immoral thing was employed to
glamorize some legal/moral product/service: serial
killers endorsing cologne; rapists, condoms; ter-
rorists, box-cutters; hit men, life insurance;
ten-year-old girls, wine coolers. For the most part,
consumer horror deters companies from pursuing
these controversial tactics, but the point is that
companies could target the small demographic
that would respond to these kinds of design statements. All you need to do is use the public-domain
list of released child molesters, and you can
market whatever you want right to them. Ditto
with court records of the incarcerated. Target
your demographic by criminal profile. The market
is amoral. Money doesn't care how it gets made.
Therefore, design doesn't care how it makes
money.[35]

3. **DissemiNation:** The means for disseminating designs
are constantly in flux. Fifty years ago, kids may

---

† We're presuming designs are used sincerely here and not as parody
or satire. I can imagine these very designs executed as satire meant
to indict the boundless immoralities of greedy companies. On
Adbusters.org, for example, you will find a satire of a Smirnoff vodka
ad that features children. Satire only works as corrective when it
presumes the reader or viewer to share a sympathetic morality.

have grown up wanting to be lithographers, but they wouldn't have grown up wanting to be web designers. Increasingly invasive means of disseminating information, entertainment, advertising, and other media await us in the future, and, in the dystopia we are imagining here, they are all fair game, distinguishable only by profitability. Environmental advertising scans your implanted I.D. chip and displays personalized messages for your eyes only, if not *in* your eyes only. Push technology shoots wirelessly into your brainchip, hijacking your optic nerve. Design will accept any forms, without a peep of misgiving.

4. **Design Designs Itself:** Designers build the software that renders the profession obsolete. The client enters the design parameters, and the smartware craps it out in milliseconds.[36] It doesn't matter whether this is empirically likely; it only matters that *you* don't matter—in this world.

After indulging in the fun of imagining the crazy scenarios of a free market fueled by the amoral efficiencies of fungible design and designers as currency and life as profit, I should emphasize what is probably pretty clear by now: that the instrumental/aesthetic & the efficient/moral overlap, entangle, enmesh, and in general get all scrunched up with each other when you tackle real designs in the real world. The conflict for designers is not represented by the paradigmatic either/or/both dialectic/synergistic showdown; it's better represented by—I hate to say it—a web, in which all threads are in tension with each other, and the trick of it all is to watch where you step—and whom you disturb.

MORAL CONTENT REVISITED. Earlier I worked my way toward the necessity of moral content from inside the designer out. Desire could be strongly felt, but that desire could take as its object immoral ends. The desire to work was an internal subjective force that needed moral orientation to enable passionate designers to distinguish promoting a KKK rally from promoting an Eminem concert.

> My object in living is to unite
> My avocation and my vocation
> As my two eyes make one in sight.

> Robert Frost, "Two Tramps in Mud Time"

There is an art to harmonizing individual desire and the good, and the opportunity to pursue that art either begins or is denied on the very practical, day-to-day level of economics. Frost recognized that one's avocation cannot survive isolated in a social world but must be linked and even modified by one's vocation, by one's work. But he also suggests that if a person were to fail to unite them, to fail to make one's joy one's work, then the person will end up half-blind.

In talking about efficiency *outside* the design, I worked my way toward the necessity of moral content from outside the designer in. Efficiency provides a means to evaluate the effectiveness of designs, but, being amoral, efficiency lacks the means to distinguish content. It can't detect immoral intents, goals, or effects. Efficiency provides designers with external incentives, rewarding efficient designs irrespective of whether the designs make money promoting Motrin or Rohypnol.[37]

Because efficiency is amoral doesn't mean it's inevitably immoral. A designer may very well regard efficiency as a value within and without the design, but efficiency is not enough by itself to ensure a good design or even a successful one. While moral content is therefore necessary, I'm not concerned here with directing anyone to a particular store in the great American morality mall, only with noting the necessity of some moral check at key decision-making nodes in the web of creator » creation » dissemination.

Creator: the creator's desire is molded by appeals to The Good, and this requires intelligent self-consciousness (The Good Mind).

Creation: this is where you consider the means of creation (sources of materials & labor, inspiration & limitation) as well as the content of the creation (the kinds of icons, images, ideas, and messages your design contains).

Dissemination: your design has to get out to the public, and this is where you examine how it's getting out there and who controls how it's getting out there.

What is maddening and fascinating about all this is how thoroughly embedded one's personality can become in one's work, whether you like it or not, whether you engage it or not, whether you dig in and resist or sit back and let it ride. Whatever you do, decisions are being made, and you are being made. The more you get used to it, the more it gets used to you, whether "it" is a bad habit or a good life.

LOST TRACK FROM THE 2004 "AMERICAN MUTT" SESSIONS, THE AESTHETIC VENDETTAS. It might seem disingenuous to clear the way for aesthetic pronouncements only to convey the futility of aesthetic pronouncements and then to go ahead and make them anyway and to again qualify them with the futility caveat. Every rule contains its breach; every beauty, its imperfection; every life, its death. Every aesthetic style is a virulent airborne spore: eventually, some mouth-breather will inhale it.

Ultimately, I feel it more pressing, and more personally urgent, to debunk the notion that one can find one's aesthetics—one's voice, style, sensibility, one's *purpose*—in the declamations of other designers. One can find inspiration in their works and words, certainly. One can be cheered; one can be disheartened. One can find artistic confirmation, and one can find new energy in angry refutation. One takes heart in the aesthetic achievements of others—honors them, appreciates them—but to achieve for one's self, one must say, "Fuck it," and get to work. The work I get to must have meaning for me to keep my interest, to justify my effort, a meaning that comes from my desires, my goals, my values, and my sense and use of history. The aesthetics of my execution are critical to the meaning. Aesthetics, like the mortality of our lives, is the container of our expression, except that designers get to shape the vessel, coloring it with truth and beauty —or with the nightmare of beauty and the flaw in truth.

I, HUMAN. There are days when I find myself shoved from an air transport, a reluctant paratrooper, flapping like commuter garbage through the jungle air, shredding the canopy of common decency and, foosballed by branches,

landing hung up and suspended over the humid decay
of a life not worth the hot water to scrub its morning face.
It is with this time-bruised face that I greet my mentor
in the mirror with a snarl-lipped *Fuck you*.

Here I am, chomping at the bit, frothing at the mouth,
unfocused energy spraying off like static electricity.
My sanity depends on work, my personhood depends on
creative output. Without good work, I'm a moody bitch
of a dog.

I don't know if my grand funks, my nihilistic moods,
have biochemistry to blame, but let's say, on these days,
ambient music ain't gonna cut it. Neither will espresso,
nor a heating pad for my neck. No, on plummeting days,
I don't care if the meek do inherit the upgrade. Let 'em
have it. Graphic design—hell, work in general—can take
a flying . . . you know what. Self-hate taints the puddle
I drink from, and pretty soon the world's image shatters
into a thousand reflecting wavelets. What of mine can put
out the fire? Let the idea burn with the thing. And let me
drown in the rain forest.

To be self-taught is to self-flagellate, to self-discipline,
to self-administer. Abstinence makes the art grow fonder.
And, time enough, I'll be back at it, out of the woods and
into the heartland, ignorant and floppy as a puppy on the
Times. There is no secret recipe for healing thyself. It's a
waiting thing. Hope is the light we switch on when the
plain facts of life are stacked and walled around us. Time
frees all fools.

No, wait. Work does. Work frees some of the fools some
of the time. Sometimes even the mutts.

END NOTES

1. I do fight against obligations to clear away time for writing and work. It's hard to be selfish when your son is running naked through the house and your daughter is asking you what the middle finger means. While I don't have the leisure to wallow in my work like a pig in mud, I do have the opportunities to steal moments here and there and make the best of them. Or not. It's a lot of hit and miss. I set the oven timer to remind me to pick up the kids from school. If I do that right, I feel like I haven't totally screwed up the day.

2. Second section in a row in which I seem to have fallen victim to masculine tropes based on the artist as suffering hero. It's likely a symptom of me working alone most of the time and therefore having only myself to talk to. In a public forum like an essay, I'm probably guilty of fronting heroic lyricism to conceal the staring-out-the-window very much anti-heroic *stasis* of most frustration. My experience with graphic design is one of working in isolation, punctuated by rare client meetings but mainly conducted in the smooth sensory deprivation of email. Getting psyched up to get out of my grand funks is something I wish I could do on command, in my head, in front of the computer, but that's the peculiar state of being in a creative depression, that by definition you can't will yourself out of it because if you could then you wouldn't really be in one—you'd just be pretending to be so you could lay claim to this suffering-hero archetype—and so I have to settle for the simulation of self-psyching-up in this essay, pretending that this is what actually happens, this psyching up to get to work, and though reading this rhetorical dramatization may psych you up (or not; you'd probably have to be in a good mood already and so this psyching-up dramatization would leverage that existing good mood as opposed to inspiring in you a brand new good mood), what happens, for me anyway, is the violent lashing out which circles back in on itself in a nutty mumbling penitent no-one-to-blame-but-myself Ben Gunn mode, a mode that ebbs away leaving me in the sadness of a waiting room, killing time until, sitting there

and idly striking keys, work pulls me out, slowly, the work forcing
me to look outside of myself and thereby extracting self-pity like a
hand-tool uprooting a weed, and so maybe it is the *process* of writing
this essay that may do the job of working me out of creative depression (even though, as in this note, I'm looking outside of myself in
order to look back into myself; trippy, though I'm hardly the first to
describe the phenomenon), but the essay doing the job is not doing
the job as a psyching up or as an exercise of the heroic da Vincian
will but, over time, as an excavation by spoonfuls.

3. This fear of having one's work stolen or copied and diluted for the
   market while you sleep is (a) probably a reasonable concern; (b)
   more likely a paranoia; or (c) definitely self-flattery. To worry "they"
   are watching you is to presume you are worth watching. The twist is
   that when you *are* worth watching, whether because you're talented
   or because you've come up with a great or popular design statement
   (T-shirt, poster, slogan, character), you will, indeed, be ripped off.
   Hence we praise the existence of intellectual-property laws, which
   enable you to make a living off your work.

   Intellectual-property rights won't, of course, always serve and
   protect you, especially not from the Big Players who are clever and
   sneaky enough to employ lawyers and writers clever and sneaky
   enough to swipe your unprotected idea without copying your pro-
   tected expression. Big Players, furthermore, try to have it both ways,
   with more protection for them, less for the little guys. Disney
   recently benefited from the 1998 Congressional extension of copyright protection from 75 to 95 years for existing and work-for-hire
   copyrights and from 50 to 70 years after the death of the author for
   new copyrights. The Sonny Bono Copyright Term Extension Act
   (1998) was upheld by the U.S. Supreme Court in *Eldred v. Ashcroft*
   (2003). Copyright for Mickey Mouse would have otherwise expired
   in 2003, and protection for Donald Duck, Pluto and Goofy in 2009.

   The extension of copyright terms applies to all of us, of course,
   not just the Big Players, but Disney, like other big companies, has the
   resources to risk pushing the infringement envelope. Many argued
   that *The Lion King* (1994) copied too closely Tezuka Osamu's *Kimba
   the White Lion* (a *manga*—based NBC TV series launched in 1966),
   and while the Japanese studio Mushi declined to file a lawsuit (osten-
   sibly in honor of Osamu's respect for Walt Disney, both men being
   deceased), Disney to this day has never credited or publicly admitted
   Osamu's work as a source. In 1993, Paul Alter was awarded damages

because Disney's *Honey, I Blew Up the Kids* (1992) infringed a story he submitted to Disney in 1980; Disney refused to write a letter of apology. In France in March of this year, Franck le Calvez lost his suit to ban sales (in France) of products from Disney's *Finding Nemo* (2003) because, the suit alleged, the Nemo character too closely resembled an orange-clown-fish character he'd created in 1995. Le Calvez unsuccessfully pitched a clown-fish screenplay to film studios for years before he authored a children's book, *Pierrot the Clown Fish* (2002), the plot of which resembles *Nemo*'s in that a young orange-and-white-striped clown fish is separated from his family. Le Calvez lost mainly because of the principle that copyright protects particular expressions, not ideas. Ironically, le Calvez was motivated to bring the lawsuit because, after *Finding Nemo* was released, French booksellers, who recognized easily enough the similarities between the two characters, refused to sell his book anymore for fear that *la Calvez* was infringing *Disney's* copyright.

[Sources: *BBC News, USA Today, The Toledo Blade.*]

4. From Aphorism 290 of Book Four, *The Gay Science*, Friedrich Nietzsche.

5. I risk sloppiness in making a comment like this because it opens the doors to discussions of identity and self-determination, of choice and free will, of what our selves are made of and how we become who we are, namely, an interrelation of genes and proteins, temperament and personality, specific circumstance and general environment. Plus there are those topographical thermal brain scans that highlight to what extent a part of the brain's neuroanatomy is triggered when a subject confronts a dilemma, say, between giving money to a panhandler and walking on to Starbucks. But knowing about the brain's operations in any depth isn't like being conscious of them as they happen, operational consciousness being the threshold requirement for then controlling the operations. Without that as-it-happens consciousness, any kind of scientific methodological knowing will only grant you the after-the-fact power of performing the equivalent of Monday-morning quarterbacking.

6. The three parts of the Platonic soul—appetite, spirit, and reason— are characterized by their own "peculiar desires": appetite for food, sex and money; spirit for honor and ambition; and reason for knowledge, truth and justice. By their objects, the desires identify the

desirers as "lovers of gain," "ambitious," or "philosophic." What is crucial, for Plato, is not the nature of desire (Plato offers here no distinctions among passion, whim, caprice, lust, preference, love) but the nature of the object of desire. Plato nearly suggests that one can merely choose among these objects of desire as one might select among figs on a plate, and Plato endorses reason, the "philosophic." Hobbes considered desire to be a general appetite and could be applied to all objects. Rousseau wrote that "human intelligence owes much to the passions" and that "it is by their activity that our reason is improved; we seek knowledge because we desire enjoyment."

To give the needed content to desire, Plato insisted on the objective good. We may be forever unable to distinguish between objective standards of what is good and our own subjective indexes, but while I want to believe the real article is a human standard, one *for* humans if not by them, I also want to believe in—and I do indeed act as if there were—an objective good external to my own conceptions and outside the subjective conceptions insisted on by other authorities.

Does it make any difference if I believe in an objective or subjective standard? When I believe in an objective standard, I am prepared to accept from start to finish that my conception is very likely wrong and that I will need constantly to do the work of reimagining new standards aimed toward this unreachable objective good. When I believe in a subjective good, I do not believe that I can ever be wrong, only inefficient, because all subjective conceptions are equally valid as choices, there being no objective (or suprasubjective) standard to judge among them. And if you argue that a suprasubjective standard is as conceivable as a subjective standard, then what follows is an infinite regression of suprasuprasuprasubjective standards, and the only way to stop this absurdity is to posit an objective standard.

Historically, political authorities (whether fascist, socialistic, democratic, or otherwise) often claim to be acting on objective standards of the good for the useful reason that citizens tend to mistakenly regard the objective as unappealable. It is this right to appeal and forever improve the standards of the good against the authorities of self, church and state that make for the difference in living under objective versus subjective standards.

[Sources: *The Republic*, Plato; *Discourse on Inequality*, Jean-Jacques Rousseau; *Leviathan*, Thomas Hobbes.]

7. For a great book on the argument for self-liberation through work, see *On Being Free*, Frithjof Bergmann (University of Notre Dame Press, 1988).

8. Vaclav Havel's speech was printed in *The New York Review of Books*, 16 December 1999.

9. David Bowie, Azar Nafisi, Freddy Adu, William H. Macy [neverfollow.com].

10. *A Wild and Crazy Guy*, Steve Martin (Warner Brothers, 1978).

11. With the decline of public space and the increase of private space, there will be more restrictions on commercial speech in private spaces like malls (which can eliminate guys in chicken suits passing out coupons as legally and swiftly as corner guitarists passing out bar flyers) and thus more restrictions on commercial speech in general. Of course, malls and other retail spaces only speak in commercial speech, and they will continue to speak loudly and clearly; it's just that the choir of storeowners will follow the rules of the local church wherein they sing. And, of course, noncommercial forms of speech will, as the trend continues, have less space in which to exist. Graphic designers, I expect, will soon be (or are) fighting serious battles against the decline of public space, and they will confront sticky issues now that hybrid public-private spaces are gaining in currency. I have noted, anecdotally, the increase in suburban retail areas mimicking the hip urban downtowns in which residential lofts are built above retail stores, and I've wondered what rules of free speech apply in these private-public hybrids and who makes these rules, especially since suburbia's sterilized, romanticized take on these loft-store hybrids is to build all of it on private real estate owned by the development group. That is, residents live in upscale apartments above Victoria's Secret and J. Crew, but all of it is built on private property, on the great expanse of what is, I guess, an outdoor mall. Design a poster for your band's gig, your next poetry reading, or your lost dog, and you'll face a crisis: where can you post it? If you elect, instead, to stand on the corner and pass it out, will the mall security guard, who lacks the authority of a city cop and may be prohibited from infringing on your free speech, have, instead, the power to evict you from your apartment?

12. Jockeys on 29 April 2004 successfully won the right to lift the ban on commercial sponsorship during the Kentucky Derby, jockeys enjoying income boosts from jersey ads and traditionalists shuddering at the slippery slope to NASCAR *(USA Today)*, and 5/6 was the day Major League Baseball Commissioner Bud Selig announced the MLB, in response to fan backlash, was no longer going to put advertisements for *Spider-Man 2* on first, second and third bases during three upcoming Athletics-Yankees games (*AP Sports*).

I'm only speculating that we will soon witness ads on diapers and big graphic designs painted on portable toilets, but it seems only a matter of time, diapers and toilets being less controversial, strangely, than athletic gear. I can envision diapers sporting ads like bumper stickers, ads for wipies, baby powder, clothes, and toys, but I can also see cute sayings printed on diapers *a la* those wisecracks on Molson beer labels: *I'm with Stinky; Don't Forget to Smell Check; Doodie Call; That's What You Get For Not Feeding Me Mushed Organic Vita-Peas® from Little Vittles, Inc.* As for portable toilets, Ericsson surely has a new captive audience, and Hollywood knows celebrities smell good anywhere.[†]

Speaking of Hollywood, I'm reminded of Bollywood: I have seen, in India, ads running at the bottom of the frame during the entirety of a rented video. These colorful, typographic, flickering things are like hybrids of Internet banner ads and the CNN ticker; they drove me out of my mind and then out of the room. Albeit willing to endure fifteen minutes of previews on DVD (and short-lived tickers during

---

[†] The fact that I even come up with new places for ads suggests there is an addictive quality to slapping every surface with a function. We wear T-shirts that promote the company that makes something other than T-shirts, and we have no qualms *paying* to wear these sandwich boards. Those cardboard coffee-girdle things now have ads on them for, like, anti-coffee-breath breath mints, which brings us to ads-on-ads, otherwise known as marketing synergy, e.g. Coca-Cola and GM partnering to give away a Chevy to the kid with the winning Coke can. Every blank surface anywhere invites you to play the game of Spank Me with an Ad. It's like being a kid on a long car ride again, seeing VW Beetles everywhere once you've decided to notice them. The satisfaction of this—not peculiar to graphic designers whose vocation and avocation is to attack the blank unpurposed surface—is a childlike one, and, as such, it fades away, like the fleeting satisfaction of shopping itself. We all want to *shop*. Who wants to *have shopped*? Once you've admired your idea for a new place to put an ad or looked in the bedroom mirror at your old ass in new pants, the mind sags, desire deflates like a balloon the day after the party, and you go looking, desperately, for new sources of pumped air—more blank surfaces to smear, more things to buy . . . .

news programs or as weather advisories), America will not, arguably, put up with this.

What we will put up with, apparently, is the movie that is itself an advertisement. I just saw a TV spot for *The Last Ride*, a Rob Cohen movie featuring a Pontiac GTO (oh, and Dennis Hopper). Here is some prose from the USA Network's website for the movie: "Twenty-five years ago they used a '69 GTO to get away. Now they'll use a new one to get even"; "a 1969 GTO that holds the key to his redemption"; "But in the hot new 350-horsepower 2004 GTO they just ripped off, they've got the drive to win." If vigilantism and grand larceny aren't your style, you can try gambling. "Be sure to enter 'The Last Ride Sweepstakes' for your chance to win a 2004 Pontiac GTO and a walk-on role in an original USA production!"

[Source: www.usanetwork.com/movies/thelastride]

13. I don't like being preached to either. I throw away any and all flyers for new books by media theorists whining about media consolidation, the end of democracy, the death of citizenship. I applaud their enthusiasm and probably would agree with much of their criticism, but the sky is not falling. I am no paranoid anarchist, no Chomskyite. The Constitution still stands, and American citizens *in toto* are no dummies. For evidence, witness 272 communities and four state legislatures resisting the federal Patriot Act by passing resolutions against it, citing its infringement of civil liberties as unconstitutional and explicitly banning its local enforcement by police and residents ("Resolving to Resist," by Elaine Scarry, *Boston Review*, Feb/Mar 2004). It's just I don't like joining groups. I don't know why. It's a reflexive aversion, ingrown as a toenail. Maybe I'm too afraid to be imprisoned in a catchall category, all my opinions packed in a roll at the end of my bunk, tin cup hung on a string tied to the bars. No, thanks. I choose loneliness (see End Note 2).

14. A complication is that a company may (a) lie terribly about a great product, in which case they violate a rule but win consumers; or (b) tell the truth about a terrible product, which violates no rule but wins no consumers. A desirable middle ground, a kind of bell curve of acceptable lies and half-truths, would be the operating ideal. However, there is reason to believe that the curve, in practice, is shaped not like a bell but like the snapped loop of a whip in which the narrow spike of the loop is concentrated at the extreme end of Risky Lies and crossing over into Actionable Lies.

15. Maybe once you surrender to the belief that nothing means anything anymore, you figure you might as well buy into the promise of immortality and instant pop-a-pill weight loss cuz why not after all go for broke? There might also be a kind of surreal relief or giddy irresponsibility that one feels (temporarily) from the very irrational act of choosing to believe in something *one knows is ridiculous*. It's like that what-the-hell feeling I get when I take the fam to Disney World. *Getting into the spirit of it all* makes me feel as silly, phony and immature as the sugar-fairy fantasy of the park itself, and this staying-in-spirit is serious labor, as hard as being an actor staying-in-character, in that it demands a constant re-suspension of disbelief and commitment to living in the false moment when every long line, cold corn dog, or barfing baby jeopardizes the happy illusion of carefree adventure. This odd human desire to journey to artificial fantasy worlds to pretend to believe you are someone you're not may somehow be seen to replicate the experience of pre-tending to be a celebrity in a movie or a rich somebody in an upscale mall. And *this* may be how we prefer to understand ourselves when we survey the graphic designs in the ads and movies and magazines all around us, that we are entertained by the illusion that we are wealthy, important, and famous. There is also the self-defensive grump we become when the thrill of the self-delusion fades, when we in mean spirits bitch and carp at how shoddily management bothered to sustain the illusion, how badly Jennifer Aniston combed her hair that day, how the wrinkles of reality were showing in the façade of dream. We seek the Customer Service desk to complain that, although we paid yesterday's admission fee, we are, today, still who we are.

16. Or maybe it's also about control. The accidental or intentional Superbowl-half-time baring of J.J.'s left breast (oops, it's the right; I just saw the photo in *Rolling Stone*) was an event over which the network barons had no (supposedly) control; they were surprised, upstaged, overpowered, made the fool. When the network otherwise has matters firmly in hand (sorry), they push the limits in limited contexts, baring boobs and butts on *NYPD Blue*, for example, or on a cable channel they own or else allowing advertisers to sneak up to the censor's lines in the sand.

    As I write this note on 13 May 2004, news outlets have been for days now employing the controlled precision of a jeweler in the placement and carefully non-graphic display of the photos of mistreated Iraqi prisoners and web-video stills of the retaliatory beheading of Halliburton employee Nick Berg. The media is clearly concerned with upsetting viewers as well as the government, but I wonder how, now that we are so far and so long into this war/occupation, such graphically violent images can still evoke shock and dismay, as if we'd been innocents up until their publication. Had we been exposed to similarly graphic wartime images throughout the past year and a half, we would surely have become, if not accustomed to their horror, then perhaps expectant of their unflinching truth. So much about the realities of the war (and even prisoner mistreatment) has been described at length in magazines and newspapers that it is surprising that we still recoil from these recent arguably less violent images. This either proves the power of the easy image over the work of imagination or else proves that most Americans don't read.[†]

17. Lots of designers do *pro bono* work, obviously, and here is a quote from one of them who offers a statement of good faith and a glimpse into sticky reality. "I continue to do design for the public good to try to present the truth, to capture the soul and to preserve integrity," says Jurek Wajdowicz, cofounder and creative director of Emerson, Wajdowicz Studios in New York. "Too often there is the fear of not upsetting anybody, anytime and anyplace. Blinding fear of not wishing to offend the boards or donors, who are sometimes brainwashed by political-correctness, often leads to the tendency of playing it safe and choosing those banal cliché solutions. It makes it even more painful when combined with historically very limited budgets." The quote comes from Rebecca Bedrossian's article, "Design for the Public Good," in the May/June 2004 issue of *Communication Arts*.

18. That which matters commercially to someone is of course important, especially to that person, but it is not the same as that which matters socially, politically, artistically, emotionally, etc. I love to do work for the small businesses of friends and relatives. They appreciate it, and I have meaning in my work on a personal level, going the extra mile for someone I care about. Designing a brochure con-

---

[†] As I write this follow-up note on 9 July 2004, there have been additional beheadings of Americans in Iraq, and none, as you might expect, have met with the same shrill pitch of public outcry that followed the initial beheading. I am sad to observe additional evidence for the proposition that the repetition of similar images inures us to content.

tributes to the success of a friend's business, and this contribution goes a little way toward helping this person pay bills, raise their kids, etc. But business is still business, and while business can be personal, our appetites hunger for more than what business alone can feed us.

19. This is as inconvenient a place as any to make glancing observations about the design sensibility of Dave Eggers and his *McSweeney's* literary journal and small press, a sensibility some feel consciously if not gleefully subverts market and design conventions. That I feel obliged to devote space to his work rather than to the work of a million other indie designers troubles me but apparently not nearly as much as Designers with a capital D are troubled by the attention that Design w/ cap D has given to Eggers. Quote: "Egger's approach is an anti-design style, flouting professional treatment... Never has a strategy so outwardly minimal been so showy and indulgent... Honoring Eggers seems less a pronunciation of design's significance than an expression of self-loathing": end quote (Kenneth Fitzgerald, "I Come to Bury Graphic Design, Not to Praise It," *Emigre* #66).

I don't know what attention Eggers has received, other than in *Print* magazine, but there must be something more. Anyway, I think his designs are tasteful if precious and ironic homages to vintage styles, and so neither the admiration nor the bitterness his designs engender compute, to me. I'm not sure what "anti-design style" is, except I bet Sagmeister's Ed Fella-influenced hand-scrawls might be anti-design or at the very least a "flouting of professional treatment," except if a designer gets paid for the work, then that makes the designer a pro in my book.

At any rate, Eggers would seem to be a good example of someone who might fit the hybrid-designer mold I'm talking about. Author of a best-selling memoir, *A Heartbreaking Work of Staggering Genius* (Simon & Schuster, 2000), Eggers launched[†] *McSweeney's*, an indie journal (and, later, a small press) with its own design statement, one consciously employing textual playfulness in fierce loyalty to the power of word over image, text and narrative as rebellion against the hegemony of icon. Self-indulgent it may be, but so are most literary journals, against which *McSwy's* positioned itself (it also positioned itself as antithetical to the slick-lit conventions adhered to by the likes of *Esquire*, for which Eggers once edited). If recent

---

† *McSweeney's* as a website and effort started around 1998, the journal followed, followed then by the press.

McSwy's illustrated book covers are any indication, Eggers has since abandoned this strategy, if he ever really regarded himself as having a strategy; he seems in his designs to behave more like a freewheeling contrarian, a practitioner of whimsy as dry as bone. Not to mention, he's not the only guy on staff. There are other writers, editors and designers atoil in the *McSwy's* factory.

However designers might feel about *McSwy's*, most young writers panted in a kind of pent-up erotic heat at its appearance, its T-shirt-and-jeans attitude crashing the tweed-only wine-and-cheese party that was the literary-journal scene of the late Nineties. Eggers, after all, is just another self-taught designer doing his own thing to create a market and serve it (which is what designers do, that whole commercial thing), and while he is now alert to the more typical frequencies of market success, as his recent projects would indicate (e.g. *The Best American Non-Required Reading,* edited by Eggers & pub'd by Houghton Mifflin Co), *McSwy's* appears to remain loyal to its contrarian mission (see *The Believer* (believermag.com)), a mission in which respect for narrative determines the design, where, in the design-game equivalent of rock/paper/scissors, Word beats Image.

Compare, for the sake of comparison, Eggers's *McSwy's* respect for text with David Carson's *Raygun's* respect for image. I was a fledgling freelance journalist when, in the mid-Nineties, *Raygun's* layouts first assaulted me with their eviscerations of text; they had clearly had quite enough of text's presumption as the royal caretaker of meaning. Ten years later (one year ago), I was a hatchling designer beaking mags and monographs and was absolutely tickled in a dirty place by Carson's designs, in which there seemed to be liberation for the designer in regarding text as object, as just another element to subordinate to the greater design. Staring at the pages of Carson's *The End of Print,* I finally understood *Raygun* was to be looked at, not read. *McSwy's*, by contrast, is meant to be read. Today I'm a writer, first and foremost, and Carson's *Raygun* designs seem to represent a phase young designers must slog through (as I did last year), the way I as a writer had to get past the tricks & tics of the postmodernists of the Sixties and Seventies.

Which is not to say that *McSwy's* is what I have in mind when I argue for The Good Mind, Narrative over Montage, or Language over Icon. *McSwy's* is Eggers's attempt. The rest of us, in contention with our own demons, will devise our own methods for romancing the white page.

20. And to the objection that commercial success in any way damages one's credibility, I reply that you're missing the very narrow point: commercial success undoes only a specific kind of credibility, the kind earned by an artist who predicates a design sensibility on an independent anti-Big Business identity and therefore sacrifices that credibility when Big Business eats his designs for breakfast. The licensing of the design to Big Business may be the prerogative of the designer, but that particular designer's previous credibility is lost to the Costs side of the balance sheet, albeit balanced by a new dependent pro-Big Business credibility on the Benefits side. This designer may also engage in a kind of dissociative self-defense mechanism whereby the qualified *I did that for Target* surrounds the wound like white blood cells and *But I did this one for me* functions as the designer's rehabilitative shot of wheat grass. Other designers who don't trade on their anti-Big Business credibility face many problems but not this one. (Yes, I've seen Shepherd Fairey's "Obey" symbol on an action figure in Target—and now you know I buy my son his Yu-Gi-Oh cards at Target.)

21. Designers may choose to turn their independent work into self-sustaining enterprises. Plugged into the market, your studio, retail outlet, or online store will be meeting the demands of an audience, enlightening and entertaining along the way. Aside from the muscles you will need to develop as you flex your economic body (not to mention hitting target muscle groups with daily reps of kissing crony ass and doing opportunistic lunches), you will need to manufacture a lot of ideas out of the factory engine your imagination has now become. Few of us are blessed with one great idea, let alone capable of daily miracles. For practical reasons rather than lofty philosophical ones, designers may choose to balance client work with independent work, the back room of independent work functioning as kind of market-testing laboratory. I'm trying to build two halves of my designing life on top of the two-part structure I've built for my writing life: writing and designing for clients by day; for me, by night. This is no great news in our civilization. People have been doing this for generations. It might be the unremarkably common lot of most artists and writers. I suspect it is desirable only to the restless and miserable minotaurs among us, to those of us eccentrics whose hearts are light on one side.

22. Eric Heiman's essay "Three Wishes," in *Emigre* 66, quotes from Rick
Poynor's article, "The Citizen Designer," published in *Trace*, in which
Poynor quotes Bennett Peji as saying, "The key to truly affecting any
group design perspective is to effect change by serving on the
board."

23. See: www.underconsideration.com/speakup/archives/001982.html.

24. If you're a designer comfortable with your current role and enjoy
a stoic acceptance of What Is, then there's nothing to talk about, and
this ambivalent hand-wringing over decoration and disposability is
driving you nuts. Much of consumer culture is disposable, from daily
journalism and television to most art, books and movies, disposability being an attribute of creatures of The Now, creatures that don't
pretend to be other than such. And most of us enjoy the decorative,
the disposable, The Now. It's just that as a graphic designer and
writer, I try to approach my work like a martial artist: I aim to strike
beyond the target.

25. I myself am still tempted by the intentionally ugly, messy, and wrong.
I think this prurient desire to fool around comes: (a) from the sudden
windshield-smashing consciousness of design as a discipline; (b)
from the realization that owning the tools of design arms you with
the power to play; and (c) from the need for self-affirmation, whereby the bold evidence of subversion grants visibility to the vain
and/or resentful. It is also, I think, an assertion of primitive humanity against dehumanization (see *The Dehumanization of Art*, by José
Ortega Y Gasset, 1968). A subsequent danger arises when the intoxicating effects of the new power wear off, leaving the dry taste of
shame, and you go looking for existing sensibilities to co-opt for
meaning and to counteract your feelings of inferiority. The co-option
of an existing sensibility is liable to doom you to accusations that
your work is pretentious and phony, especially where stylistic self-
consciousness is part of the conventional inauthentic life that a
given "raw" sensibility rejects. Self-styling one's work as, say, punk
or punk-inspired is like trying to be the Green Day of design (Green
Day being the Baby Gap of punk). (I like Green Day, and probably
because I'm not a punk, simulacra being palatable for the tastes of
a tourist.)

26. There is a pretty standard though relatively undiscussed no-no in fiction writing, and that is literalization of metaphor. Metaphor, analogy, and simile require leaps of the imagination, and it is during that suspension wherein one considers the likeness of two unlike things that the mind expands its capacity for analysis and abstraction. (Parsing similarities and differences is the basis of all legal argument; lawyers rely on analogy to argue whether or not facts of the present case are similar enough to the facts of past cases to be governed by a particular rule.) To literalize metaphor is to collapse a comparison into flat acceptance, to hobble the imagination. It makes for real groaners.

   The old saying meant to call out someone's hypocrisy features a pot calling a kettle black. This is a metaphor, a bit of homespun fantasy meant to rib a blowhard. A pot did not actually come to life and, like the Archie Bunker of kitchenware, vent pent-up sexual frustration by slinging racial slurs at steamy little plump little hot little Ms. Teapot. A modern story that literalizes and extends this metaphor would likely cast a Fanny Faucet who leaks informative gossip, a Prosecutor Long Spoon who distorts the truth and turns facts upside down, a Defense Attorney Paring Knife whose sharp intellect is matched only by his cutting sarcasm, and a Judge Colander past whom nothing gets (except water). Mildly amusing but the stuff of political cartoonists and *Sesame Street*. It ages badly.

   Literalizing metaphor is something designers should try to avoid at all costs, mainly because it's so much easier for a purveyor of images to get away with it before there's even time to consider how the inevitable regret of having-not-really-gotten-away-with-it will taste. It's easy to be pleased with oneself at first but hard to live with these designs afterward. They fall flat instantly, like a corpse you propped up.

   But don't listen to me. Here's proof of my point about the futility of aesthetic guidelines or really any kind of guidelines. "The Ceiling," a short story by Kevin Brockmeier, is a perfect example of the literalization of a metaphor. The sky is falling. Literally. A big dark surface is descending and squishing suburban residents. Nearly every creative-writing teacher in the country should have cringed. Instead, this story was published by *McSwy's* and won First Prize in the 2002 O'Henry Awards.

   ["The Ceiling" can be read online: www.randomhouse.com/bold-type/ohenry/0902/brockmeier_ceiling.html]

27. I realize that history, too, like culture, can be looted, and it should be clear I'm not talking about propping up a mummy in your poster and calling it "a knowing reference to ancient Egypt." Don't look to *Lord of the Dance* for the startling truths about Celtic history. And don't look just yet to my designs for evidence of all these theories in action. I design to learn, and learn by design. I usually live with my designs, the ones I care about, for weeks or months, returning to them again and again, until I'm convinced I can, indeed, live with them. Time is a luxury of working on my own projects, unpressured by deadlines.

I'm more comfortable putting the pedal of theory to the metal of practice when it comes to writing essays and fiction. I may not be any more successful there either ("'American Mutt' is the self-indulgence of an amateur who presumes to tell us what he thinks we don't already know"; see § SUBVERTING MARKET CONVENTIONS), but as a writer, I am more experienced and confident. Writing out my ideas in this essay is a way of excavating design assumptions buried in my brain, dusting them off and examining them for redeeming qualities, the way I also do, continually, in my writing. It is perhaps in writing out my own ideas about design, and in examining closely my own process, that I will enjoy the most benefits (see *instrumental value*, § ANOTHER DIGRESSION, BACKSLIDING INTO AESTHETICS). This may sound like a Design 101 exercise (I wouldn't know), except I suspect you wouldn't have much to write about until you've practiced design for a few years, in which case I may be making a big deal out of something as dull as what goes on in company retreats and design seminars (again, wouldn't know).

28. The article, "Nightmare on Madison Avenue," *Fortune*, 28 June 2004, describes a recent trend crushing the profit margins of big ad firms. The new thing is that big companies have forced ad firms to change the way they bill for services. "The recession brought about more change on Madison Avenue in four years than the industry has seen in four decades. Until recently many agencies pocketed 15% of the cost of the media they purchased for their clients. In the past five years big advertisers like Chrysler and Unilever have done away with commissions entirely. Instead, the vast majority of clients now pay fees based on an agency's labor costs. Worse, agencies must often negotiate not with the clients' CEOs but with procurement officials who are used to dealing with vendors of staplers and filing cabinets." The balance of power, continues the article, has shifted from the

advertising creators to the clients' media buyers, who care a lot
about negotiating low fees and care very little about great ad ideas.

29. Say an administrator wants their crony to win a bid, but there's a
problem: another company tends to submit lower bids and, according
to the explicit rules of the game, wins the contracts. What can the
administrator do? He simply prevents the other company from par-
ticipating in the bid process at all. If they aren't allowed to play, then
they can't win. Now the administrator can ensure their crony wins
the bid, even though the administrator's company is now paying
more for the job.

30. This is also why there is so much cross-marketing; marketers hope
that a person will transfer some of their already-established good
feelings for the movie/show/magazine/etc. onto their insinuated
product/service. Additionally, one might argue that this kind of thing
—going with the already-proven—is pretty much what happens right
now, especially with risk-averse clients, and that an Adjusted
Profitability Index (or other measure of the past or future market
performance of a design/designer) won't in practice change the
client/designer relationship. My guess, though, is that even risk-
friendly clients will now be influenced, whether they like it or not,
by the existence of such instrumental indexes and will be compelled
at least to justify index-defiant decisions. Oh and let's not forget
that even supposedly "objective" scales like these will be subject
to manipulation in favor of the manipulators (see previous two
footnotes).

31. Applying the psychological phenomenon of hindsight bias to a
particular economic example, you find a healthy sane person would
sacrifice their life for a sum far, far greater than the price tag the
same person would affix to another poor sap who has already died.
People can apply the indices of life-valuation that insurance companies use quite soberly on other people who have, say, died accidentally
in a house fire, but the same people go $$$-crazy when it comes
to sacrificing their own still-in-progress life. People instinctively feel
the qualitative difference between the cost of giving something up
and the compensation for having already lost something.

32. "Is economics a humanist discipline?" asked Robert Heilbroner, in
a 1994 essay, "Taking the Measure of Economics," published in

Culturefront and reprinted in *Harper's*. "The answer is yes, but for
a reason I think many economists would reject. The reason is that
economics, at its base, is inextricably connected with the exercise
of social power, and power in all its forms and uses is inextricably
connected with social values and moral judgments."

33. Valuing everything in $ to calculate costs vs. benefits makes every-
    thing into fungible goods. Anything worth, say, $1 million is equiva-
    lent, whether a house, a Picasso, or a human life. Burn your neighbor's
    house down? Pay $1 million. Kill somebody? Hand over the Picasso,
    and you're free to go. Embezzle $1 mil? Well, that's equivalent to an
    average human life; so either pay it back or swab your arm for the
    lethal injection. (Historically, criminalizing financial malfeasance
    resulted in the construction of debtor's prisons, but residence inside
    them was unjustly the lot of the poor who suffered at the mercy of
    the ruthless rich; imagine white-collar criminals today executed for
    squandering hundreds of millions of dollars; they'd probably say,
    hell, it was worth the try.) It isn't efficiency that prevents this dollar
    equivalency. Economics is strictly amoral. It's morality, secular jus-
    tice, that pulls this weight. In many cases, we are willingly ignorant
    of our devil's bargain. We're willing to sacrifice human lives for, say,
    cars and highways, the defense of our country, the use of prescrip-
    tion drugs—anything that benefits society as a whole but may cost
    tens of thousands of lives. We can even predict how many lives will
    be lost to a new drug, new construction, new car, etc., because it
    happens every year. We keep doing it anyway. The moral monstrosity
    of this is controlled, to extents, by federal and state standards,
    voluntary and involuntary product recalls, lawsuits, even insurance
    against unlikely but possible worst-case scenarios, etc., but the point
    is that overall we as individuals just don't consider the bargains we
    have made for our cars, drugs and other luxuries until tragedy befalls
    us specifically and our moral outrage finds its voice.

34. The power balance in the real-world designer/client relationship, of
    course, works differently. The client has the need first, sets parame-
    ters, and approves or rejects ideas of yours. You can't be responsible
    for effects if you aren't responsible for the final product. It's infuri-
    ating to realize the client will still blame you, associate your
    good-faith effort with the aroma of what is mostly their own failure.
    Try telling the client who writes your checks, whose business you
    want to win again, that it's their fault.

35. And because we are focusing on money and the market, I have not mentioned the moral issues designers have faced working under oppressive, violent, sadistic, and/or genocidal governments or political movements. In literature, the writer's political orientation is usually judged harshly in hindsight; occasionally, great writers are treated to generous apologies for their failings, but the works of many lesser writers are sentenced, without a second thought, to oblivion. Graphic designers who have created, say, propaganda for oppressive communist or fascist regimes or for wrongheaded socialist ones or even for British imperialism or American global hegemony are not judged—that I've noticed—for their faults of stupidity, ignorance, cowardice, or intellectual naïveté. All works of art and design retain historical significance. It's critical reception that's the interesting issue. When, if ever, should the content that informs a design so undermine its credibility that it prohibits any consideration of the aesthetics of its form? My knee-jerk response is, "Never." My sense is that the works (not the creators) should be judged on form and content both, no matter what (probably not even great aesthetics can rehabilitate ideologically crippled propaganda), and that it will be their critics who will be judged on the wisdom of their selectivity and the intellectual power of their arguments.

36. After I thought of this idea, I read what Sagmeister had to say about the same idea in his monograph, *Made You Look.* "All that professional, good-looking, well-produced pretty fluff is going to be generated by sophisticated computer programs. You type in the client, select a format and a style, the program lets you choose from a vast list of visual clichés, downloads a picture selection, aligns everything and sends the files to the printer."

    Beyond the conjecture, consider the reality, and not the prevalence of software templates but, rather, the extents to which stock-photography-and-video companies are going today. Plus there are companies that now provide stock TV ads for political campaigns (read it in "Dumb and Dumber," an article in *The Atlantic,* July 2004). It isn't much of a leap from customized stock to personalized schlock. Couple that with the increasing insistence on rock-bottom prices big corporations are demanding from the big advertising firms (see End Note 28), and the slide into automated ads seems only a matter of time. Coming soon: *Creativity as commodity.*

37. Flunitrazepam (a benzodiazepine), a tranquilizer stronger than valium, has been called the "date-rape drug," noted commonly around 1996 (www.emergency.com/roofies.htm). Taking effect in half an hour or less and lasting several hours, the drug induces sedation, amnesia, muscle relaxation, and a slowing of psychomotor responses.

NEW design titles from Princeton Architectural Press

100% EVIL
NICHOLAS BLECHMAN AND
CHRISTOPH NIEMANN
WITH AN INTRODUCTION
BY CHIP KIDD

APRIL 2005
5 X 6 IN / 176 PP
176 2-COLOR ILLUSTRATIONS
PAPERBACK
$14.95 / £9.99 / €14.50

"There's evil in the world."
—George W. Bush

And lots of it. The question is, just what does it look like?
A politician? An ex-girlfriend? Your landlord? Your boss?
In this hilarious, disturbing, quirky, and brilliant little book,
noted illustrators Nicholas Blechman (*Empire*) and Christoph
Niemann present a catalog of their own misanthropic
imaginings. *100% Evil* is a thoughtful, comical, and—at
times—joyful book that just goes to show that sometimes
it's good to be bad.

CLASSIC BOOK JACKETS
THE LEGACY OF
GEORGE SALTER
THOMAS HANSEN
WITH A FOREWORD BY MILTON GLASER

JANUARY 2005
8.25 X 9.75 IN / 200 PP
224 COLOR ILLUSTRATIONS
PAPERBACK
$35.00 / £25.00 / €36.00

For more than forty years, the beautifully drawn and lettered covers of George Salter have served as elegant windows into the works of such revered authors as Albert Camus, John Dos Passos, Jack London, and Thomas Mann. Salter had the rare ability to reduce the illustrated dust jacket—a new part of the book package—to its essential elements. He could visually evoke—with typography, calligraphy, and pictorial imagery—the contents of any given book.

Classic Book Jackets includes more than 200 reproductions of Salter's finest works, and a complete catalog of his jackets, designs, layouts, and lettering for the book trade.

CUBE
DAVID MORROW GUTHRIE

FEBRUARY 2005
6 X 7 IN / 176 PP
160 COLOR ILLUSTRATIONS
HARDCOVER
$20.00 / £14.99 / €20.00

The cube is one of nature's purest, most basic forms. But it can be altogether more complicated? Imagine you're asked to create a cube using materials such as plywood, bamboo, foam, hay, chopped up telephone books, or even strands of chicken wire.

That's the design exercise architect David Morrow Guthrie gives his students each year at Rice University, and the results, over 50 of which are presented in this handy little block of a book, will inspire any designer who is looking for ideas and inspiration, whether from elemental forms or innovative ways of using materials.

DESIGN BRIEF SERIES from Princeton Architectural Press

THINKING WITH TYPE
A CRITICAL GUIDE FOR DESIGNERS, WRITERS, EDITORS, AND STUDENTS
ELLEN LUPTON

7 X 8.5 IN / 176 PP
100 COLOR ILLUSTRATIONS
PAPERBACK
$19.95 / £14.99 / €20.00

The organization of letters on a blank sheet—or screen—is the most basic challenge facing anyone who practices design. What type of font to use? How big? How should those letters, words, and paragraphs be aligned, spaced, ordered, shaped, and otherwise manipulated? In this groundbreaking new primer, leading design educator and historian Ellen Lupton provides clear and concise guidance for anyone learning or brushing up on their typographic skills.

Thinking with Type is divided into three sections: letter, text, and grid. Each section begins with an easy-to-grasp essay that reviews historical, technological, and theoretical concepts and is then followed by a set of practical exercises that bring the material reviewed to life. Sections conclude with examples of work by leading practitioners that demonstrate creative possibilities (along with some classic no-nos to avoid).

GEOMETRY OF DESIGN
STUDIES IN PROPORTION AND COMPOSITION
KIMBERLY ELAM

7 X 8 IN / 176 PP
92 B+W ILLUSTRATIONS
4 COLOR PLATES
PAPERBACK
$16.95 / £11.95 / €16.50

Kimberly Elam lends insight and coherence to the design process by exploring the visual relationships that have foundations in mathematics as well as the essential qualities of life. *Geometry of Design* takes a close look at a broad range of twentieth-century examples of design, architecture, and illustration—from the Barcelona chair to the Musica Viva poster, from the Braun hand-blender to the Conico kettle—revealing the underlying geometric structures in their compositions.

Explanations and techniques of visual analysis make *Geometry of Design* a must-have for anyone involved in graphic arts.

GRID SYSTEMS
PRINCIPLES OF ORGANIZING TYPE
KIMBERLY ELAM

7 X 8 IN / 120 PP
200 B+W ILLUSTRATIONS
45 COLOR PLATES
PAPERBACK
$16.95 / £12.99 / €17.00

In her best-selling *Geometry of Design*, Kimberly Elam shows how geometrical systems underlie many of the visual relationships that make for good design. Now, Elam brings the same keen eye and clear explanations to bear on the most prevalent (and maybe least understood) system of visual organization: the grid.

Filled with extensive research and more than 100 informative examples from the Bauhaus to Nike ads, *Grid Systems* provides a rich, easy-to-understand overview and demonstrates a step-by-step approach to typographic composition. Any designer, educator, or student will benefit greatly from this elegant book, chock-a-block full of colorful examples, helpful vellum overlays, and Elam's insightful analysis.

Grid Systems
Kimberly Elam

Filled with an expansive range of twentieth-century examples of design, from Jan Tschichold's brochure for *Die Neue Typographie* to Bauhaus graphics to a Nike catalog, *Grid Systems* provides a rich, easy-to-understand overview of the grid and demonstrates a step-by-step approach to typographic composition. It reveals design strategies that transcend simple function and reductionist recipes to allow grids to become a means of truly dynamic communication.

ELEMENTS OF DESIGN
ROWENA REED KOSTELLOW
AND THE STRUCTURE
OF VISUAL RELATIONSHIPS
GAIL GREET HANNAH

7 X 8 IN / 160 PP
200 B+W ILLUSTRATIONS
150 COLOR PLATES
PAPERBACK
$16.95 / £11.95 / €16.50

Rowena Reed Kostellow taught industrial design at Pratt Institute for more than 50 years and her teaching legacy has changed the face of American design. This instructive and invaluable book reconstructs the series of exercises that led Kostellow's students from the manipulation of simple forms to the creation of complex solutions to difficult design problems. It includes her exercises and commentary along with selected student solutions, and concludes with examples of work from former students who became leaders in the field, including such well-known figures as Tucker Viemeister, Ralph Applebaum, Ted Muehling, and many others.

A hands-on book design students and designers alike will welcome.

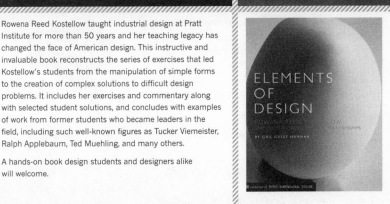

ELEMENTS
OF
DESIGN
ROWENA REED KOSTELLOW ... OW ... RELATIONSHIPS
BY GAIL GREET HANNAH

THE SCHOOL OF THREE-DIMENSIONAL DESIGN

✳ ✳

THIS ISSUE OF *EMIGRE* WAS SET IN

FAIRPLEX

A Family of Types Designed by Zuzana Licko

LICENSED AND DISTRIBUTED BY EMIGRE FONTS

✳ ✳

NARROW BOOK & BOLD $95.00	M	*M*	**M**	***M***
WIDE BOOK & BOLD $95.00	M	*M*	**M**	***M***
NARROW MEDIUM & BLACK $95.00	M	*M*	**M**	***M***
WIDE MEDIUM & BLACK $95.00	M	*M*	**M**	***M***

✳ ✳

BUY ALL 16 FAIRPLEX FONTS FOR $299

AND SAVE $81

✳ ✳

Fairplex was inspired by features found in models ranging from the S. F. Giants logo to Garamond. With tapered serifs that become more distinct and decorative as size and weight increases, and an overall low contrast, Fairplex is designed to function as both an animated headline font and highly practical text typeface.

✳ ✳

WWW.EMIGRE.COM

✳ ✳

FAIRPLEX NARROW BOOK, **BOLD** & *ITALICS* 10/13 POINT

If one is inclined to *wonder* at first how so many dwellers came to be in the loneliest land that ever came out of GOD's hands, what they do there and why stay, one does not wonder so much after having lived there. None other than this long brown land lays such a hold on the affections. The rainbow hills, the tender bluish mists, the *luminous radiance of the spring*, have the lotus charm. They trick the sense of time, so that once inhabiting there you always mean to go away without quite realizing that you have not done it.

FAIRPLEX WIDE BOOK, **BOLD** & *ITALICS* 10/13 POINT

If one is inclined to *wonder* at first how so many dwellers came to be in the loneliest land that ever came out of GOD's hands, what they do there and why stay, one does not wonder so much after having lived there. None other than this long brown land lays such a hold on the affections. The rainbow hills, the tender bluish mists, *the luminous radiance of the spring*, have the lotus charm. They trick the sense of time, so that once inhabiting there you always mean to go away without quite realizing that you have not done it.

FAIRPLEX NARROW MEDIUM, **BLACK** & *ITALICS* 10/13 POINT

Men who have *lived* there, miners and cattle-men, will tell you this, not so fluently, but emphatically, cursing the land and going back to it. For one thing there is the divinest, cleanest air to be breathed anywhere in GODs world. Some day the world will understand that, and the little oases on the windy tops of hills will harbor for healing its ailing, house-weary broods. There is promise there of *great wealth in ores and earths*, which is no wealth by reason of being so far removed from water and workable conditions, but men are bewitched by it and tempted to try the impossible.

FAIRPLEX WIDE MEDIUM, **BLACK** & *ITALICS* 10/13 POINT

Men who have *lived* there, miners and cattle-men, will tell you this, not so fluently, but emphatically, cursing the land and going back to it. For one thing there is the divinest, cleanest air to be breathed anywhere in GOD's world. Some day the world will understand that, and the little oases on the windy tops of hills will harbor for healing its ailing, house-weary broods. There is promise there of *great wealth in ores and earths*, which is no wealth by reason of being so far removed from water and workable conditions, but men are bewitched by it and tempted to try the impossible.

Text excerpted from *The Land of Little Rain* by Mary Austin. Houghton, Mifflin & Company, 1903.

Emigre Product Info

Emigre Magazine

Emigre is published twice a year with issues coming out in February and August. As of February, 2004, *Emigre* has discontinued selling subscriptions, and will sell only single issues.

Back Issues

Many back issues are available at the regular cover price or less. Collectors' issues (those which are available in very limited quantities) start at $25.

Miscellaneous

Emigre also offers T-shirts, artists' books, posters, wrapping paper, music, ceramics, and the always popular Sampler Bag containing a collection of Emigre goodies.

Emigre Type Catalog

To order a copy of the comprehensive *Emigre Type Catalog* go to: www.emigre.com//EmigreCatalog.php

Mailing List

Help us keep our email and mailing lists up to date. You can change your email address, or take yourself off our mailing list at: www.emigre.com/work/acct_login.php

How to Order Emigre Fonts & Products

Order On-line
www.emigre.com
Fonts are available for immediate download, all other items are shipped within five business days.

Order by Fax
Print out a faxable order form at: www.emigre.com/EFax.php
Fax anytime: **(530) 756-1300**

Order by Mail
Enclose payment by check or charge your credit card.
All checks must be payable through a US bank, in US dollars.
Mail to:
EMIGRE
1700 SHATTUCK AVE., #307
BERKELEY, CA 94709
U.S.A.

Emigre News
Add yourself to the *Emigre News* emailing list. We use *Emigre News* to help keep you informed of new products, services, and special limited offers. To sign up go to: **www.emigre.com/enews**